NO PHONES ALLOWED!

BIG BOOK

OF FAMILY GAMES

Original

101

FAMILY
& GROUP
GAMES

That Don't Need Charging!

BRAD BERGER

To Taylor and Rebekah

FAMILIUS

Copyright © 2019 by Brad Berger
All rights reserved.

Published by Familius LLC, www.familius.com

Familius books are available at special discounts for bulk purchases, whether
for sales promotions or for family or corporate use. For more information,
contact Familius Sales at 559-876-2170 or email orders@familius.com.

Library of Congress Cataloging-in-Publication Data
2018966233

Print ISBN 9781641701334
Ebook ISBN 9781641701716

Printed in China

Edited by Katie Hale and Alison Strobel
Cover design by David Miles
Book design by Brooke Jorden

10 9 8 7 6 5 4 3 2

First Edition

WHO SHOULD USE THIS BOOK . . .

FAMILIES

FRIENDS

A GROUP OF STRANGERS

WORK ASSOCIATES AND COLLEAGUES

TEACHERS AND STUDENTS

SORORITY SISTERS

FRATERNITY BROTHERS

ROOMMATES

TEAMMATES

CELLMATES

PRIMATES

MEAT EATERS

VEGETARIANS

PEOPLE FROM SWEDEN

REALLY SKINNY BASKETBALL PLAYERS

BALLROOM DANCERS

SUMO WRESTLERS

SCIENCE NERDS

LATE-NIGHT TALK SHOW HOSTS

EXCESSIVELY HAPPY PEOPLE

CHEESE ENTHUSIASTS

GARGOYLES AND WIZARDS
(WITH COLLEGE DEGREES)

PEOPLE NAMED PHIL
(BEFORE IT WAS POPULAR TO CALL YOUR SON "PHIL")

HOBBITS WHO CAN NEVER
FIGURE OUT WHAT TO WEAR

PEOPLE WHO EAT WAY TOO MUCH CELERY

ZOMBIES WHO TALK BEHIND YOUR BACK

AND . . . THE GRANDCHILDREN
OF PROFESSIONAL BOWLERS

FOR EVERYONE ELSE,
JUST MAKE IT A GREAT GIFT

When we are alone in our cars on long road trips, there are various ways we all like to pass the time. Some of us listen to music or podcasts, others talk on the phone, and many of us just take the time to think, enjoy the scenery, and complain about the other drivers.

Me? Well, I think about a new game I want to invent for my friends and family to try out at our next game night. First, I think about a specific experience I want to create. Then, I think about the different people in my gamer groups of varying ages, interests, and personalities. I think about how they would all approach the game and react to it, and the rules I would have to put in place to make for the best possible overall experience. This initial process could take anywhere from one to five hours. Once I have the concept all set, it's time for Game Night! Most of the time, I don't tell anyone I'm trying a new game out. They just assume it is one I have played with others before and they are simply next in line. If it hits the bull's-eye the first time, I'm halfway there and I give it a few more rounds with different people and different size groups, perhaps changing the rules slightly based on the reactions and feedback from the first attempt. If it doesn't work perfectly but the concept still has legs, I make necessary changes and give it another shot. Otherwise, I may scrap the concept altogether and it's back to the drawing board and another long drive. At some point, a new game is created with lots of fun times to be had in the years to come.

So, why tell you all of this? Because the 101 games in this book have all been tested and played many times and have produced the best memories with the hundreds of people in my focus groups over the course of several years. These are my absolute favorites!

What you have in your possession is a book of games that accomplishes three of my main goals when bringing people together:

1. **Disconnection from Technology:** For five minutes or five hours, you will all be engaged without the distractions of your phones and tech devices.
2. **Convenience:** In one book you have a choice of many different kinds of social games for groups of all ages and sizes.
3. **Adaptability:** With these games, *you* control the categories and themes based on the personalities and interests of your specific group.

SELECT THE EXPERIENCE YOU WANT

///

> **THIS BOOK IS BROKEN OUT INTO TEN CHAPTERS, EACH INCLUDING GAMES THAT PROVIDE A SPECIFIC TYPE OF GAMING EXPERIENCE.**

- **Predictions:** Games that require you to match your lists with the lists of the other players in your group. How well can you predict what everyone will say? (See page 1.)
- **Discovery:** Games that lead to discovering a lot about the past, present, current goals, and specific interests of everyone in your group. (See page 63.)
- **Creativity:** Games that give you a launchpad for getting your creative juices flowing, with the ultimate objective of impressing the judges and making people laugh. (See page 109.)
- **Performance:** Games that allow you to show the group you missed your calling as an actor and should be the next in line for a big role on Broadway. (See page 145.)

- **Deception:** Games that test your ability to completely change your personality and pretend to be someone else in the room. (See page 167.)
- **Strategy:** Games that require you to come up with the ideal plan based on your perception of the knowledge of each individual in your specific group. (See page 185.)
- **Speed:** Games that challenge your ability to think quickly and come up with the answer before anyone else. (See page 239.)
- **Memory:** Games that offer fun ways to test how well you can remember what you have seen or heard. (See page 281.)
- **Puzzle solving:** Fun competitions where teams work together to solve puzzles. (See page 315.)
- **Athletic:** One multi-event, Olympic-style friends and family competition that brings together people of all ages and athletic abilities to compete in an epic battle. (See page 329.)

HOW TO USE
THIS BOOK

//

IMPORTANT TIPS ON HOW TO ORGANIZE YOUR SOCIAL GAMING EXPERIENCE:

MATERIALS:

All you will need to play most of these games are pens or pencils and paper. Ideally, every player should have his or her own pad. I like to purchase the small pads you find at many pharmacies and office or school supply stores. Every player puts his name on the pad, and that's his game book for the day, night, or week. For some of these games, we recommend index cards over paper. You'll understand why as you read the game instructions. Some games don't require anything at all besides the players themselves.

PATIENCE:

Some of these games will take you less than five minutes to figure out. Others will demand slightly more time, and some will require you to read the instructions a few times and to play several practice rounds before your group gets the hang of it. Just stick with it!

The most important advice I can give to anyone organizing a group to play any of these games is to be well-prepared with what kind of game or games you want to play before even introducing the idea. In other words, make sure you have your pads and writing instruments all ready. Read the instructions of the games you want to play and understand them before you begin to teach everyone else. Be the game director and scorekeeper. The games always run more smoothly when you have a designated organizer.

BEWARE OF OVERLY COMPETITIVE BILLY

///

One of the things that has fascinated me when playing all kinds of games with people throughout the years is how quickly you realize a person's competitive nature. It really doesn't matter whether you are playing tic-tac-toe or basketball. If someone is ultracompetitive, you will usually figure it out within a few minutes. In the same sense, when someone couldn't care less about winning or losing, that is quite obvious as well.

All of the games in this book are social games. The fun (for the most part) is all about the journey and much less about who wins the game. Most of the memories are about the things people say and the fun new things you discover about each other. Still, all of the games have rules and it is important to follow them in order for the true experience to be realized. And, of course, there are winners and losers.

However, whenever I get a group of people together and there are people I don't know, in addition to going over the rules and winning objective, I make absolutely sure to emphasize the true meaning of the game and what kind of approach will make for the best experience. This way, if there are any of what I call "Quadrant Four" competitors, they may end up toning it down once they realize there isn't a

Lifetime Achievement Award for being the only one to figure out whether Uncle Joe's story was true or false . . . and that nobody will care if they were the only one to not figure it out.

So, who is a "Quadrant Four" competitor? In order to understand those people, we should probably start with "Quadrant One":

QUADRANT ONE COMPETITORS

These are the least competitive people you will ever meet. When these people are invited to play a game, many of them will actually show up, but that's mostly because they are just happy to be included. Many times, you'll notice that Quadrant One competitors have no idea they are even playing a game. They really don't care about the rules. Often, Quadrant One competitors will get up from the table and leave in the middle of a crucial game moment and come back several minutes later. This isn't because they are rude people; it's just that another activity popped into their heads and it was far more interesting at the time. Although it is difficult to play games with Quadrant Ones, often they are a pleasure to be around because all they want to do is be around everyone else. Still, these people are often looked at by real competitors as having two heads. Few understand them other than perhaps some Quadrant Two competitors, but even Quadrant Twos will scratch their heads in amazement sometimes. How a Quadrant One and a Quadrant Four can even coexist is beyond me. It's quite amusing to see an actual couple like that. How is it even possible they got together?

QUADRANT TWO COMPETITORS

A Quadrant Two competitor actually wants to know the rules of the game, unlike the Quadrant Ones. Quadrant Two competitors like playing games and want everyone to have a good time. However, unlike Quadrant One competitors, Quadrant Two competitors are very aware of the Quadrant Threes and Fours. They recognize them right away and will absolutely let them win if they feel winning is more important to them—which, of course, it always is. I love playing with Quadrant Twos—and that's not because they will let a Three like me win, but because they are simply never going to cross the line and aren't going to lose focus either.

QUADRANT THREE COMPETITORS

Unless you are a baby, a Quadrant Three competitor won't let you win. Simple as that. These are highly competitive people who give 100 percent every time, unlike the Quadrant Two competitors who fluctuate between seventy and ninety percent and the Quadrant Ones who don't even know what I'm talking about. Quadrant Three competitors will play as hard at Scrabble as they play rugby or football. Quadrant Three competitors like to play mostly with other Quadrant Three competitors. This is really the best scenario for a Quadrant Three—everyone playing hard, no nonsense, and no letting anyone win. The Threes do get along with the Twos, but get very frustrated with the Ones and Fours. Win or lose, when the game is over, a Quadrant Three competitor will get over it and move on pretty quickly—usually within five minutes. Quadrant Threes won't complain too much about losing and won't boast too much when they win.

QUADRANT FOUR COMPETITORS

Finally, we have our Quadrant Fours, the group this guide is really all about.

If you are a Quadrant Four and you're still reading this, don't worry, we still love you, but there's probably little hope for you.

So, what's the best way to describe a Quadrant Four? A Quadrant Four is a mixed bag of goodies. Have you ever experienced a moment where you tell a group of people, "We're all going to play a new game," and one person starts to break out into a full sweat? Almost definitely a Quadrant Four. He's wondering if there's a chance he can lose at whatever is about to be announced, and that would be a total disaster in the life of a Quadrant Four. For a Quadrant Four, a loss is pretty much equivalent to the world coming to an end. Many times, a Quadrant Four will decline to even play a game because he knows himself and also knows the experience will be awful for everyone. As opposed to Quadrant Ones leaving the table randomly at a crucial moment in a game without even realizing it, you can often pinpoint the exact moment a Quadrant Four is about to disappear by recognizing the look on his face when he realizes there's a good chance he can't win. Rather than sticking around for everyone to see it, he'll just slip away unannounced and never come back. The great irony is that although Quadrant Ones and Fours are from two different planets, at times they will be forced to hang out with each other while the Twos and Threes finish the game.

Some Quadrant Fours will actually cheat if they are out of winning options. Other Quadrant Fours will cause a distraction just to take the focus off of whatever it is they are embarrassed about. As can be expected, many people are hesitant to play games with Quadrant Four competitors, with the possible exception of Quadrant Three competitors, who will gain the most satisfaction out of beating them and are often more willing to take the risk of getting beaten and hearing about it for years to come. Unlike a Quadrant Three who knows when a Quadrant Two is letting her win, a Quadrant Four has no idea when a Quadrant Two is handing him the victory, because that kind of behavior doesn't compute. To a

Quadrant Four, everyone is playing their hardest when he is winning, which makes him the best at whatever it is. He's the greatest and he'll make sure nobody forgets it.

So, which one are you? When I speak about this with people, there's almost always an admission of where they belong. Sometimes people like to say they cross over the different quadrants from time to time. That's perfectly fair. Some things are certain, however: A Quadrant One will typically never be anything else. Twos and Threes may flirt with each other. Threes may cross over to the dark side from time to time, and as for the Fours, well . . . they simply require a lot of tender loving care.

In the end, I find playing games with people of all competitive Quadrants incredibly interesting, and at times quite humorous when they are all playing together. As long as you're aware of who you're dealing with and can laugh it off, any group of people can come together and have fun.

CONTENTS

hese games are a great way to get your group quickly into game-playing mode! They always lead to conversations about specific topics and what each individual in your group considers to be the most popular choices or common knowledge on many different subjects or themes. For most of the games in this chapter, the objective is simple: match your list with the lists of the other players. Do you think alike?

The first seven games in this chapter are similar, but *not* the same! Each of these games has a different twist which will greatly influence the choices you make. For these games, you will be asked to come up with your own categories. The specific categories you select will ultimately be based on the personalities and interests of each individual in your group. However, here are 200 suggestions to help get you started:

200 SAMPLE CATEGORIES FOR MIND READER GAMES 1–7:

1. Popular team sports
2. Popular male first names
3. Popular female first names
4. Popular Olympic sports
5. Popular vegetables
6. Popular fruits

7. The most popular cities people like to visit outside of North America
8. Popular New York City attractions
9. Popular Broadway shows
10. Common things you find in a kitchen
11. Common things you find in a bathroom
12. Popular science fiction movies
13. Popular comedy movies
14. Musical instruments
15. Common types of pasta noodles (not including spaghetti)
16. Things that are green
17. Things that are yellow
18. Things that are red
19. Sports teams with animal names
20. Popular vacation destinations
21. Popular fast-food restaurants
22. Popular sports movies
23. Words that begin with the prefixes "prob-," "prof-," or "prog-"
24. Common soups served at a restaurant
25. Famous people named Robert or Bob
26. Famous people named Jennifer or Jessica
27. Famous people named John or Joe
28. Popular stores in the mall
29. Popular languages to learn
30. Popular animated movies
31. Popular comedians
32. Popular breakfast cereals
33. Popular rock bands through the ages
34. Famous painters
35. Popular magazines
36. Famous female singers
37. Famous male singers

38. Famous world leaders
39. Things people buy at a hardware store
40. Things people buy at a supermarket
41. Popular board games
42. Popular automobile manufacturers
43. Things that smell bad
44. Things that smell great
45. Famous actors, actresses, singers, or athletes who have gotten themselves into trouble
46. People who have made the biggest impact on the world in the past 100 years (positive or negative)
47. Popular TV dramas
48. Popular TV comedies
49. Songs with the word "love" in the title
50. The world's most well-known large corporations
51. Popular horror films
52. Popular Disney characters
53. Things that are sharp (not including a knife)
54. Common sports injuries
55. Cities in the world that begin with the letter "S"
56. Cities in the world that begin with the letter "M"
57. Common foods at a barbecue
58. Hollywood actors many people consider to be good-looking
59. Hollywood actresses many people consider to be good-looking
60. Popular authors
61. Popular house pets (not including dogs or cats)
62. Common things found in a garage
63. Popular exercise routines
64. Common restaurant chains
65. Types of balls
66. Types of dressings
67. Herbs or spices

68. Popular ways to eat chicken (or specific chicken dishes)
69. Types of fish
70. Words or phrases many English speakers know in other languages
71. Popular zoo animals
72. Words that rhyme with "dark"
73. Things that are hot
74. Things that are cold
75. Oscar-winning movies
76. Famous basketball players
77. Famous baseball players
78. Famous football players
79. The world's greatest inventions
80. Well-known shoe brands
81. Well-known brands of beer
82. Common brands of chocolate bars
83. Popular desserts ordered in a restaurant
84. Popular ice cream flavors
85. Famous stadiums, arenas, or concert halls
86. Things that are scary
87. Types of breads
88. The most popular types of cookies
89. Things people spend money on
90. Psychological thriller movies
91. Popular reality TV shows
92. Common illnesses
93. Popular TV show hosts
94. Popular kinds of sandwiches
95. Popular male actors of all time no longer living
96. Popular female actresses of all time no longer living
97. Things that break
98. Things you wear
99. Common snacks

100. Countries with the hottest climates

101. Common park activities

102. Famous people named Michael or Matt

103. Hotel chains

104. Popular Muppets

105. Types of pies

106. Casino games

107. Famous actors who were *Saturday Night Live* cast members

108. Common professions

109. Well-known rivers, seas, or lakes

110. Countries in Africa

111. Popular movies with sequels

112. Famous superheroes

113. Water activities

114. Things people do while wearing a helmet

115. Famous presidents

116. The highest-grossing movies of all time

117. Popular games played indoors

118. Popular cable TV channels

119. Frequently used words that begin with the letter "Q"

120. Frequently used words that begin with the letter "Z"

121. Adjectives used to describe people in a positive way

122. Adjectives used to describe people in a negative way

123. Famous people who became famous when they were kids

124. Common street signs

125. Popular American sports teams

126. Cities or countries that begin with the letter "C"

127. Actors who play tough guys in movies

128. Activities or sports you probably shouldn't do naked

129. Things people do before they go to bed

130. Common words with a silent "K" or "B"

131. Well-known Canadian cities

132. The most well-known dance styles

133. Things you open, turn on, or start

134. Types of juices

135. Words that begin with "wh-"

136. Popular individual (as opposed to team) sports

137. Well-known bugs and insects

138. Dangerous sports

139. Types of street signs

140. Common texting abbreviations

141. Well-known universities

142. Places where people wait in long lines

143. Cities or countries that begin with the letter "P"

144. The most popular cheeses

145. Types of salads

146. Weather terms (not including "cold" or "hot")

147. Common words or phrases used by announcers at a baseball game

148. Famous blond celebrities

149. Things you would find at a gym

150. The most famous country singers of all time

151. Types of cakes

152. Foods or dishes that are really messy to eat

153. Names people give their pet dogs and cats

154. Common names for streets in the United States

155. The most popular TV shows about solving crimes

156. Popular western movies

157. Wealthy people in the world

158. Successful college sports teams

159. Top brands of soda (not including Coke and Pepsi)

160. Common allergies
161. World cities or regions that have had major historical events occur in the last 100 years
162. Movies or TV shows starring or about an animal or animals
163. Popular card games
164. Hotels with casinos
165. Famous brothers and sisters, fathers and sons, or mothers and daughters
166. Uniform numbers of famous athletes
167. Specific vacation destinations with beautiful beaches
168. Popular US cities to visit (not including New York, Chicago, or LA)
169. Popular European cities to visit that are not in France, Italy, or the UK
170. Famous people named Bill or William
171. Popular romance movies
172. Popular cities or towns for skiing
173. The greatest tennis players of all time (male or female)
174. Famous fashion designers
175. Holidays on a calendar in the United States
176. Cities that begin with "T" or "R"
177. Popular sauces
178. Common items used for cleaning
179. Popular singers/musicians who have acted in movies
180. Popular companies/brands associated with technology
181. Popular game shows
182. Popular TV shows before 1980
183. The most popular video games of all time
184. Well-known actors/actresses who have played animated characters in movies
185. Famous movie directors

186. Countries with large populations (not including China)

187. Things people collect

188. US cities with only one or two professional teams in the four major US sports

189. Cities that have hosted the Olympics

190. Reasons kids get into trouble at school

191. Well-known movie villains

192. Popular dog breeds

193. Frequently used three-letter words in the English language

194. Common last names in the United States

195. The most recognizable buildings in the world

196. Popular brands of cleaning products

197. Well-known chemical elements

198. Famous celebrity couples

199. Famous actor pairs who have worked together in more than one movie

200. Popular college degrees

MINDREADERS

1. Famous people named Charlize
2. Things you do when locked in a closet
3. Really friendly cannibals
4. Well-known tall couples who are afraid of heights
5. What your dog thinks when you leave the house
6. Songs about Roxanne or Levon
7. Conservative drag queens
8. People in your group with bad breath
9. Things vampires do in their spare time
10. Things people say when they run out of things to say

POPULAR

3+
PLAYERS

///

DO YOU HAVE A PULSE ON POPULAR OPINION?

PREPARATION:

Each player comes up with five categories that will lead to many possible answers (see pages 1–8 for ideas) and places them in a hat or face-down on a table mixed in with all of the others.

OBJECTIVE:

A player's goal is to match his or her selections with as many of the other players' selections as possible in every chosen category. When a category is selected, players list the items that they think will be the most popular choices, meaning the items in a given category they predict will be on most of the lists of the players in the group. The more players a person matches for each selection, the more points he earns.

GAME TIME:

Players take turns drawing categories out of the hat without looking. Once Player 1 selects a random category for the first round, he decides how many items (from five to ten) everyone will list in that category.

Once the category is announced, no players may speak until all players have completed their lists. Allow players two minutes to create their lists. If a player cannot finish his list in that time, that player will have fewer chances to score points.

Once every player has read his list and received points for all matched items, each player gives his total points for the round to the scorekeeper, and play continues as Player 2 draws a new category. If she picks a category from the hat that was submitted by more than one person and has already been used, she picks again.

SCORING:

Once all players have completed their lists, players take turns going around the room announcing items they have listed one at a time. Players earn 1 point for every person who matched one of their items—including a point for themselves. (For example, if a player matches an item on her list with three other players, all four players receive 4 points for that item.) Add up the points for each item to determine the total for that category. Players receive no points for an item if they were the only one who listed it.

Let's say you have a game of seven players. Player 1 goes first and randomly selects from the hat the category "Things that are green." He then decides that he wants everyone to list eight things that are green. Players have two minutes to list their eight items.

> **Note:** If you can't come up with eight, then you simply will have fewer chances to score in the round than those who have eight listed. It doesn't mean you won't get a high score, but ideally, you want to give yourself the best chance by listing the maximum number of items requested.

After every player writes down up to eight items that are green in the time allotted, players take turns reading the items on their lists. Player 1 goes first. If his first item is "broccoli," and five out of the seven players (including Player 1) had "broccoli" on their lists, then all five of those players receive 5 points (1 point per player). The other two players receive nothing.

Player 2 goes next and reads one of her items. If that item is "grass" and three of the seven players said "grass," then those three get 3 points for "grass." Player 3 then reads one of his items, and so on, until every player reads all of his green things. Again, there is no need to repeat an item on your list that has already been said since that item has already been scored.

No points are awarded if only one player has a specific item. In other words, if Player 4 has "traffic light" on her list and nobody else wrote "traffic light," Player 4 would not get any points for that item. If one other player had "traffic light," he and Player 4 would both get 2 points.

MAJORITY RULES

PICK THE NUMBER ONE
ANSWER IN EVERY CATEGORY

PREPARATION:

Each player comes up with five categories that will lead to many possible answers (see pages 1–8 for ideas) and places them in a hat or face-down on a table mixed in with all of the others. If you play more than a few rounds of this game, each player may have to add categories, depending upon how many total players you have.

OBJECTIVE:

A player's goal is to come up with the number one or majority answer in as many of the ten categories selected in each round as possible. A player can only score in this game if her one choice is the most popular.

GAME TIME:

One player is elected in each round to randomly draw ten categories from the hat. One at a time, she reads a category, and then each player has no more than thirty seconds to write down what she thinks the majority of the players will write as the most obvious or popular answer. Players may not list more than one.

EXAMPLE:

If the category is "Common Things You Find in a Kitchen," you must write down what you believe most people in your group will think is the most common thing you would find in a kitchen.

Important: Once the first of the ten categories is announced, no players may speak until all ten categories are read. Once all ten categories are read and everyone has their lists complete, answers are revealed and points are awarded. Then another player randomly selects ten new categories for round two. A category cannot be repeated. If the player selects a category that has already been played in a previous round, he discards it and selects again.

SCORING:

The player who selected the categories goes first and announces what she had for the first category. Everyone who matches her selection raises his hand. Other answers are revealed after that, and the most popular answer is determined. If a player's answer is in the majority, the player wins a point for that category. The next player will announce what he had for the second category, and the other players will share their answers to discover the majority answer. Play continues until the majority answer is determined for all ten categories.

Example:

With six players in the game, if the category is "Common Things Found in a Kitchen" and three players wrote "refrigerator," two players wrote "sink," and one player wrote "dishwasher", *only* the three players who wrote "refrigerator" earn a point.

In Case of a Tie:

If there is a tie for the majority, all of those players receive a point. For example, if two players had "refrigerator," two players had "sink," one player had "dishwasher," and one player wrote "oven," then the players who had "refrigerator" and "sink" all get a point.

IMPORTANT RULE:

No points are awarded for a category if everyone has a different answer. So, all players can get a point in a category if everyone has the same answer, but nobody gets a point if no players match.

BUYING TIME

CHOOSE THE PLAYER YOU THINK WILL SCORE BIG!

PREPARATION:

Each player comes up with five categories that will lead to many possible answers (see pages 1–8 for ideas) and places them in a hat or face-down on a table mixed in with all of the others.

OBJECTIVE:

The goal for the person who selects the category and keeps the timer is to determine who he thinks will be the biggest scorer in that category. The goal for everyone else is to match selections with as many of the other players as possible in each category. The more players a person matches for each selection, the more points scored. The player who selected the category receives a specific amount of points based on how close he was to his prediction. (See scoring.)

GAME TIME:

Player 1 randomly selects a category from the hat. He doesn't tell anyone the category yet. First, he writes down on a piece of paper who he thinks will score the most points for the category and places it face-down in front of him without revealing it to anyone. Then he sets a timer for thirty seconds, announces the category, and starts the timer. The remaining players now have thirty seconds to list as many items in the category as possible, up to ten. Each player wants to list the items he thinks will be the most popular choices—in other words, items he thinks will be on most of the lists of the players in the group. When thirty seconds are up, Player 1 says, "Pens down!" Now every player has to make a choice. If comfortable with their list, they can stop right there and get bonus points before the point scoring even begins. The amount of bonus points is equivalent to the number of total players in the game. For example, if there are six players in the game, those players who stop after the first thirty seconds each start with six points. Or, players can buy an additional ninety seconds to add to or modify their list. Players who elect to do that forfeit the bonus points. For everyone who buys the ninety additional seconds, Player 1 starts the ninety-second timer. Everyone else who didn't buy time must sit and wait. Remember, each player can only list up to ten items.

Important: Once the category is announced, no players may speak until all players have completed their lists.

Once the ninety additional seconds are up, answers are revealed and points are awarded. Then Player 2 selects a random category from the hat, makes a prediction on which player she feels will score big, and starts the timer for everyone else to make their lists in round two.

Tip: If you are not at all comfortable with the category, the wise decision may be to just take the bonus points instead of wasting ninety more seconds trying to think of items you may never come up with—even if you had another ten minutes. On the other hand, if you know the category but aren't great under the thirty-second pressure, buy more time so you can not only add to your list, but potentially make a few changes if you have more than ten items in mind.

EXAMPLE:

If the category is "The Most Well-Known Dance Styles," you must write down as many of the most common dance styles (up to ten) you believe most people will have on their lists. If after thirty seconds you only have four listed and you feel with another ninety seconds you can add some more and get closer to ten for many more potential points, elect to forego the bonus points and buy the extra time.

SCORING:

Once the ninety additional seconds are up (if at least one person bought the extra time) and all players have completed their lists, players take turns sharing one item on their lists at a time. Players earn one point for every person who matched one of their items, including one point for themselves. For example, with the category above, if a player had "Salsa" on his list of common dance styles and three other people had "Salsa" on their lists, all four players receive 4 points for "Salsa." If another player announces she has "Hip-Hop" on her list and two other players also have "Hip-Hop," then all three players get 3 points for "Hip-Hop." No points for players who are the only one with an item. Players add up their points for each item to determine their total for that category. If they didn't buy the time, they add the bonus points to their total. If they bought the time, no bonus points. Once all points are awarded for every item on all lists, Player 1 flips over his paper and reveals who he thought would have the most points for his category. If he was correct, he gets the same amount of points as that person, plus 10 bonus points for the correct prediction! If that person came in second, he gets the exact same amount as that person—no bonus points. Finally, if that person didn't place first or second, Player 1 gets the amount of points that person received *minus* 20!

Important: The player selecting the category must make his prediction before he announces the category. You may not announce the category and then see who is confident in it before you make your official guess as to the player you believe has the potential to score the most points. In addition, once the category is announced, the thirty-second timer must start immediately.

PARTNERS

4+
PLAYERS

IS YOUR TEAM UP FOR THE CHALLENGE?

PREPARATION:

Each player comes up with five categories that will lead to many possible answers (see pages 1–8 for ideas) and places them in a hat or face-down on a table mixed in with all of the others. Player 1 begins by picking a certain number of categories out of the hat. That number is determined by dividing the number of players in the game by two. (For instance, if there are six players in the game, Player 1 would pick out three categories.) If there is an odd number of players in the game, then round down. (In other words, with nine players, round down to eight and pick out four categories.) Player 1 flips over the categories for everyone to see and then determines which players she is going to pair up in each category.

Note: Player 1 has a distinct advantage in her round: she gets to select her partner and their category first. Player 1 then pairs up the remaining players and assigns each pair one of the remaining categories. If there are an odd number of players in the game, one player (call him the "extra player") will not be paired up initially in each round, but he will still contribute and earn or lose points in the round like everyone else. (More on that under "With an Odd Number of Players.")

OBJECTIVE:

Once categories and pairs have been chosen, each player must attempt to match the items related to the category on her list with the items on her partner's list.

GAME TIME:

With categories assigned, all pairs begin making their lists at the same time. Both players in each pairing must write down a total of three items each. Each player is trying to write down the three most popular or common items in her team's chosen category. Essentially, the three items she feels are going to be written down by her partner. Once the selection of categories begins, no talking is allowed amongst the players trying to match until every player is finished making her list. Everyone has a total of two minutes to make their lists of three items. Once everyone is finished making their lists, scoring begins.

SCORING:

If a pair gets at least two matches in their category, each player in the pair earns 5 points. If a pair gets fewer than two matches, everyone else in the game earns 5 points for the pair's lack of success. If a pair gets all three to match, they get 20 points each.

EXAMPLE:

Let's say you have a game of six players. Player 1 goes first and picks out three random categories: "Common Board Games," "Popular Stores in the Mall," and "Famous People

Named Bill or William." First, she decides who in the round should be her partner and which of these three categories will be easiest for them to match. Let's say she chooses Player 2 as her partner and "Common Board Games" as their category. She then decides which pairs of players will have the most difficulty matching their lists for "Popular Stores in the Mall" and "Famous People Named Bill or William."

She assigns Players 3 and 5 and Players 4 and 6 to be partners, and all pairs begin making their lists according to their assigned categories. Player 1 and Player 2 try to predict which board games the other will put on her list.

WITH AN ODD NUMBER OF PLAYERS:

Once the teams are determined, the extra player who was not selected by Player 1 for a team for the round decides who in the game he wants to help. He can help only one person in the game try to match with her partner. He can choose anyone he likes, and if the team is successful, he will receive the same number of points as the people on the team he helps. Therefore, in most cases, he will choose to help a player on the team he feels has the greatest potential to match all three. The extra player will also benefit from the lack of success of any other team he didn't help. In other words, he receives 5 points every time another team doesn't match at least two items—same as the paired players.

MATCH JACK

3+
PLAYERS

HOW WELL CAN YOU MATCH YOUR SELECTIONS WITH ANOTHER PLAYER IN YOUR GROUP?

PREPARATION:

Each player comes up with five categories that will lead to many possible answers (see pages 1–8 for ideas) and places them in a hat or face-down on a table mixed in with all of the others.

OBJECTIVE:

The objective is to list items that will match with the items on the list of *one specific player*.

GAME TIME:

Player 2 picks three random categories from the hat, discards two, and reads aloud the one she selects for Player 1. All players have two minutes to make a list of as many items in that category as possible that will match with Player 1's list (up to ten items). Player 1 also makes his list of up to ten items at the same time.

Note: It is important for Player 1 to list as many items as possible (up to ten) on his turn in order to earn as many points as possible. More on that under "Scoring."

When two minutes are up, Player 1 announces how many items he has on his list. The rest of the players must now narrow their lists down to the same number as Player 1. Players cannot have any more listed than Player 1 has. During this time, players with fewer items than Player 1 cannot add items; they just wait while the rest of the players narrow down their lists.

When all players' items have been compared to Player 1's list, all of the players, including Player 1, add up the points they earned for Player 1's round (see "Scoring").

Next, Player 3 selects three categories from the hat and selects one of them for Player 2, and everyone tries to match Player 2's list.

EXAMPLE:

Player 2 picks "Popular Olympic Sports," "Ice Cream Flavors," and "Popular Magazines" out of the hat. She decides to select "Popular Olympic Sports" for Player 1 and puts the other two back in the hat. The timer then starts for everyone. When two minutes are up, Player 1 announces that he has eight items listed. Every player must now make sure they have no more than eight popular Olympic sports on their lists. So, if Player 2 had ten items on her list, she must *cross out* two of them. Once everyone is done finalizing their lists of a maximum of eight, Player 1 reveals his eight items.

SCORING:

Points are awarded based on the number of matched items. Player 1 receives 5 points for each correct match with every other player in the game. All other players receive 10 points for every item they matched on the list of Player 1. For instance, in the above example with "Popular Olympic Sports," everyone had to match with Player 1. If Player 3 matched six items correctly with Player 1, Player 3 would get 60 points and Player 1 would get 30 points for Player 3's answers. If Player 5 matched four items correctly with Player 1, Player 5 would get 40 points and Player 1 would get 20 points. Player 1 simply adds up the points he earned from each other player for his grand total on that round.

STRATEGY:

In this game, when it is your turn for everyone to match your list to earn points, you have the opportunity to really increase your point total! For example, if there are six players in the game besides you and you match five items with every one of them, you receive 150 points (25 × 6) for your round, while everyone else will only receive 50 points each. However, you are at the mercy of the person selecting the category for you. That person doesn't necessarily want you to earn a lot of points if you are already one of the point leaders. Therefore, out of the three categories he pulls out of the hat, he may select the one he feels you will have the most difficult time listing popular items. On the other hand, that person also wants to score big on your round if he feels he can pick a category where you both will be on the same page more than the other players. If he matches seven items with you and everyone else matches four or fewer, he receives 70 points while the other players get 40 or fewer for that round. It is a tricky decision for the player selecting the category. Usually that player will select the category *he* is most familiar with.

My Matches with Everyone

Richie: 3 Matches = 15

David: 5 Matches = 25

Meri: 4 Matches = 20

Michael: 6 Matches = 30

Jill: 5 Matches = 25

Abe: 3 Matches = 15

Total Points: (130)

BETTING ON BOB

//

RISK IT ALL OR
HEDGE YOUR BETS

PREPARATION:

Each player comes up with five categories that will lead to many possible answers (see pages 1–8 for ideas) and places them in a hat or face-down on a table mixed in with all of the others.

OBJECTIVE:

The goal for Player 1 is to list the one most popular item in the category that she feels most people will bet on in order to earn points from multiple players. The goal for the other players is to score as many points as possible (max 20) for each round by organizing their bets wisely. Players' bets for each round are based on how confident they are in the selection the key player will make and how much of a risk they are willing to take.

GAME TIME:

Player 1 selects a random category from the hat and announces it. Player 1 will eventually *only* choose the *one* most popular item she can think of in that category. However,

Players 2, 3, and 4 will first each say one item in the category that Player 1 definitely cannot choose. They cannot converse about it. Each must simply announce an item that cannot be used one at a time. Once the three items that are off-limits are determined, Player 1 writes her selection on a piece of paper and turns it over. She may not change her selection. Player 1 then remains silent and gives no hints at all as all other players list up to four items they feel Player 1 might have put down. Each player can bet a combined 20 points on his items, but no more than four items can be in play.

In other words, if the category Player 1 selected is "Team Sports," and "Basketball," "Baseball," and "Football" have been determined by Players 2, 3, and 4 to be off-limits, one player might bet 5 points on "Hockey," 5 points on "Soccer," 5 points on "Volleyball," and 5 points on "Rugby." Another player might put all 20 points on "Hockey." It is entirely up to the players how they want to bet their 20 points, but they can only place up to four bets. Just keep in mind Player 1 cannot choose any of the three items that were off-limits. So, after all final lists are made and everyone has their bets, each player reveals what he bet, how many points he allocated to each of his guesses, and he can even explain his thinking. Player 1 remains silent while everyone has a chance to talk about how he split up his bets. Bets may not be changed once they have been determined. After everyone reveals their bets, Player 1 then reveals her selection.

SCORING:

First of all, nobody loses points in this game. You are betting with house points, so to speak.

Player 1 earns the same amount of points as the players who win bets. So, if in the example above, Player 1 chose to go with "Hockey" and Player 2 had bet 10 points on "Hockey," both Player 1 and Player 2 would earn 10 points.

If Player 3 bet 4 points on "Hockey," he and Player 1 would each earn 4 points. If Player 6 bet all 20 points on "Hockey," he and Player 1 would each earn 20 points. If nobody else had "Hockey" on their lists, Player 1 totals her score. In this case, it would be 34 for that round. (20 + 10 + 4). Therefore, the player selecting the category has the chance to score big. The other players can only score a maximum of 20 points in the round if they take the big risk, while Player 1 can score multiple times according to how many players match her.

Player 2 then selects a random category and Players 3, 4, and 5 each mention an item which will be off-limits.

NOBODY HAD THAT

//

> ## FOOL YOUR FRIENDS INTO THINKING YOUR ITEM WAS ON ONE OF THEIR LISTS

PREPARATION:

Each player comes up with five categories that will lead to many possible answers (see pages 1–9 for ideas) and places them in a hat or face-down on a table mixed in with all of the others.

OBJECTIVE:

The goal for Player 1 is to come up with an item that wasn't submitted by anyone but that everyone else will think was actually submitted by at least one of the players. The two goals for everyone else are to

1. Figure out which of the items wasn't submitted by anyone else and was actually added by Player 1.
2. Not submit an item that others will select.

GAME TIME:

Player 1 goes first and selects a random category from the hat and announces it. He then must announce one item from the category which is off-limits. Nobody can list that item. Every other player in the game must now write down the *one* most popular item she can think of in that category (other than the one which is off-limits) on one piece of paper. You may only write one item in the category!

Very Important: Do not let anyone see what you write!

Players write their name on the paper and hand it to Player 1. Player 1 collects all of the papers and examines them carefully, without letting anyone see the answers. If he can't understand an item someone wrote, he must hand the paper back to that person for clarification without anyone else seeing. Nobody may talk during this process or provide any hints about what they submitted. Player 1 now has no more than sixty seconds to add *one* item which he feels is the most popular item in the category that nobody submitted! He writes that item down on another piece of paper, adds it to the pile of submissions, and mixes them up. He then discards all duplicates. In other words, if more than one person submitted the same item, he keeps one of those papers and places the duplicates face-down in front of him or to the side where nobody has a chance to see what he discarded. He then reads all of the different items submitted, including his own, in random order, and everyone has to figure out which one he added.

For example, let's say there are six players in the game, the category selected by Player 1 is "Popular Fruits," and Player 1 says that nobody can list "Apple." Players 2–6 must now each submit one popular fruit other than "Apple" to Player 1. Player 1 looks at them all and gets rid of any duplicates without letting anyone see them. Let's say there are a total of four different fruits submitted by the five other players: "Strawberry," "Banana," "Watermelon," and "Orange." He then has to think of a popular fruit that wasn't provided.

Player 1 decides to go with "Grapes," writes it on a piece of paper, and adds it to the list. Player 1 then reads aloud the five total fruits in random order.

Every other player must now try to figure out which item is the one that Player 1 added. Players write down their answers on a piece of paper. Again, no hints or talking during this process. Once all answers are written down, each player reveals his guess at once.

SCORING:

Player 1 earns 5 points for every player he fools and doesn't guess his item. If a player guesses correctly, that player earns 10 points. In the example above, every player who guessed "Grapes" would earn 10 points in that round, and Player 1 would earn 5 points for every player that *didn't* guess "Grapes." If a player guesses incorrectly, he doesn't lose any points. However, for every player who guesses an item that *you* submitted to Player 1, you lose 5 points! For example, if Player 3 submitted "Orange" in the "Popular Fruits" category above, and Players 4 and 5 thought that "Orange" was the one Player 1 added, Player 3 would lose 10 points! (5 × 2) If two players submitted "Orange," then both of those players would lose the points.

STRATEGY:

The player who picks the category wants to do his best to add the most popular item that nobody submitted so most people will think it was actually submitted by at least one person. This is that player's opportunity to earn big points.

Of course, he can take a risk and use reverse psychology, picking an odd choice to make people think there's no way he would have added it and that someone else in the group must have come up with it. That can be a big risk, though. When it is your turn to select a category and add your item, you want to earn as many points as possible by picking an obvious item in the category that everyone missed. The more obvious it is, the more people will feel someone must have listed it.

For players submitting their items, you want to list the most popular item you can think of in the category. In the above example, you didn't want anyone to think that your fruit was the one Player 1 added. If your fruit was chosen by multiple players, you would lose many points! Therefore, for each round you want to avoid having your item be suspected by anyone as "unpopular enough" for nobody to list. This point deduction rule was put in place to prevent people from submitting unpopular items to throw people off. If everyone did that, there would be no point in announcing a category. You could simply write anything down.

Important: In this game, you want to select categories that will lead to *many* different answers for the most popular item. There shouldn't be an obvious top two. For example, in a category such as "Popular Ice Cream Flavors," most people would simply list "Chocolate" and "Vanilla." That would make it very difficult for the player trying to fool everyone. If he eliminates Vanilla, everyone may just list chocolate and vice versa. If he eliminates Strawberry, everyone would probably just list chocolate or vanilla. So again, submit categories where there aren't an obvious top two.

NEXT:

Player 2 selects a category, announces it to the group, collects all of the items and then adds an item nobody listed. Everyone takes a turn trying to fool the group!

WHAT WOULD MOST PEOPLE SAY?

4+
PLAYERS

///

> **MAKE IT DIFFICULT FOR EVERYONE TO CHOOSE FROM THREE GREAT OPTIONS!**

PREPARATION:

Each player comes up with a multiple-choice question and three specific, equally popular answers. Possible questions might sound like these: "If you could only have one type of food for the rest of your life, what would it be? (A) Italian, (B) Chinese, or (C) sushi." Or, "Which of these three vacation options would be your first choice? (A) Hawaii, (B) an African safari, or (C) Paris."

OBJECTIVE:

The player leading each round must come up with a question and three answers that will make it difficult for the other players in the game to determine the obvious popular choice, while the other players try to guess the most popular choices for everyone else's questions.

GAME TIME:

Starting with Player 1, all players take turns revealing their multiple-choice questions and answers. Each player in the game (including the player who came up with the question) then silently writes down the answer she thinks most people would say.

> **Important:** Note that your answer isn't necessarily what *you* would say. Try to predict what you think *most* people would say—people in general, but more importantly, the people in the game! Of course, never let anyone see your answers until they are all revealed— and do not peek!

Once Player 1 has posed her question and all answers have been written down, all players reveal their answers. The person who asks each question should keep track of how many people voted for each possible answer. When all the answers are revealed, tally the scores for that question. Play continues as Player 2 asks his question, and so on until all players have had a chance to ask their questions.

SCORING:

Each player (including the player who wrote the question) gets the amount of points equivalent to how many people had her same answer. So, if three people have the same answer, each of those three players gets 3 points. If four people have the same answer, each of those four players gets 4 points, and so on. No points are awarded if a player was the only one to pick a specific answer. Therefore, nobody ever gets one point in a given round. In addition, the player asking the question gets *no points* if everyone in the game has the same answer! The answering players get points, but the asking player gets nothing!

Finally, the player who asked the question has the opportunity to earn bonus points. The number of bonus points is equal to the total number of players in the game. If no single answer from the three possibilities was chosen by more than half of the players, the player who asked the question gets the bonus points.

Important: These bonus points can give a real advantage in the game, so when you write your question, be sure that your three options are all equally popular rather than having one overwhelmingly obvious choice that might lead more than half the players to choose it.

At the end of the game—whether after one round or multiple rounds with different questions from each player—the player with the most points wins.

EXAMPLE:

Let's say there are six players in the game. Player 1 asks, "If you could only have one type of food for the rest of your life, what would it be? (A) Italian, (B) Chinese, or (C) sushi." Everyone, including Player 1, reveals their answers at once, holding up a paper that says A, B, or C. Three players chose "Chinese," two players chose "Italian," and one chose "sushi." Player 1 earns 6 bonus points because none of the three possible food choices was chosen by more than half (in this case, more than three) of the players. The players who chose "Chinese" each earned 3 points; the players who chose "Italian" each earned 2 points; the player who chose "sushi" did not earn any points because he did not match with anyone. After the scores are tallied, the game moves on to Player 2's question. He asks, "Which of these three vacation options would be your first choice? (A) Hawaii, (B) an African safari, or (C) Paris." All six players put down "Hawaii," so the five other players each earn 6 points, but Player 2 earns no points because all six players in the game picked the same answer to his question.

GREAT MINDS THINK ALIKE

3+ PLAYERS

WHICH PEOPLE IN YOUR GROUP ARE THE MOST CONNECTED?

PREPARATION:

Every player in the game must make a grid of five rows across and five columns down for a total of twenty-five boxes. Number the boxes from one to twenty-five going horizontally across the top row, then down to the second, and so on. In the end, the number one should be in the upper left-hand corner, the number five in the upper right-hand corner, the number twenty-one in the bottom left-hand corner, and the number twenty-five in the bottom right-hand corner.

On a separate piece of paper, write each player's name, leaving enough space next to each name for tally marks.

OBJECTIVE:

For each of twenty-five random words, players must guess the most popular word that comes to everyone's mind each time. If players connect well with most of the other players in the group, they will have a good chance of being part of the winning couple or team.

Play begins with Player 1 saying a random word. (Any word goes; just make sure it is a real word and nothing that is a private joke between two of the people in the game.) Let's say Player 1 says "Pepper." In box number 1, each player (including Player 1) writes a word she thinks everyone else will say after hearing "Pepper." Often, that word may simply be the first word that comes to mind. Players must not let anyone see their answer! Then Player 2 says a *different* randomly chosen word, and in box number 2, all players write a word associated with that word. Play continues until all twenty-five boxes are complete. (It is not necessary for all players to have an equal number of turns coming up with a word for the group.)

Once all twenty-five boxes are filled in, all players reveal their answers to each box one by one, starting with box number one, and players will start to see which players are on the same mental wavelength.

SCORING:

In the end, players will see how well they matched with each individual player in the game on all twenty-five answers by tallying matches. The couple with the most matches wins.

EXAMPLE:

For instance, for the word "Pepper," it is reasonable to think many people might write "Salt." If Player 1 wrote salt and two other people in the game also wrote salt, then Player 1 puts a tally mark next to those players' names on his list. With these two people, Player 1 already has one match each. Everyone does the same with their answers. For box number two, Player 2 chose "Army." If four players wrote "Navy," those four would put tally marks next to the other three players they matched.

Tip: Words like "Pepper" and "Army" may create a lot of matching. Your words certainly don't have to be that easy. It's really up to each individual player to choose his own word each time it is his turn.

If, at the end of the game, Player 2 and Player 6 matched nine answers out of the twenty-five and no two other players matched as many, they win. Credit can also be given to second- and third-place couples.

Important: In the event of a tie for first place after twenty-five words, simply add another row of boxes and five more words. Everyone competes in the extra round, and the couples in third or fourth place now have the chance to catch up and perhaps win! (These added rows can really heighten the competition, because now most players know who they need to match in order to win.) Keep adding one row at a time until a winning couple is revealed once the matches for the last word in the row are determined.

TEAM PLAY OPTION

It can become difficult to keep track of everyone you match for each word with a lot of players, so we recommend following the "Team Play" option if there are more than six players in the game. With team play, players are all still rotating around the room and using the same twenty-five words, just like with individual play. The difference is that the scoring becomes a point system.

Teams of three or four players try to match each other rather than the group. In a team of three players, the team receives 2 points if two members match on a word and 3 points if all three answers match.

A team of four players can also earn 2 points if only two of the team members in the group match on a word. However, a team of four players cannot earn 3 points! Even if three of the four players match on a word, they still only earn 2 points. Instead, a team of four players has the chance to earn 4 points if:

- All four players' answers match on a word
- Two team members match on the same word, and the other two members match on the same word. (For example, if the initial word was "Ice" and two people on the team of four wrote "Cold" and the other two wrote "Cube," then your team would earn 4 points.)

Note: This rule is put in place to make it fairer for teams of three players to compete against teams of four players. Teams of four simply have an advantage over teams of three since they have more opportunities for matches. Therefore, this adjusted scoring slightly removes the advantage.

1 cube	2 moon	3 green	4 ball	5 chocolate
6 winter	7 hockey	8 orange	9 foot	10 wave
11 jaws	12 city	13 holiday	14 food	15 Halloween
16 Spain	17 spoon	18 sweet	19 drive	20 frame
21 tennis	22 casino	23 lava	24 Christmas	25 cat

Jennifer ✓✓✓✓
Mike ✓✓✓✓✓✓
Debbie ✓✓✓✓✓✓✓✓✓
Louis ✓✓✓✓✓✓
Rachel ✓✓✓✓✓✓
Greg ✓✓✓✓✓✓✓✓
Phil ✓✓✓
Megan ✓✓✓✓✓✓✓

HOW MANY NAMES CAN YOU MATCH AND HOW MUCH OF A RISK ARE YOU WILLING TO TAKE?

PREPARATION:

For each round of this game, one player comes up with ten sets of initials of famous people and writes them down. The player must first decide which category she wants to play. She can select "Entertainment" (actors, singers, performers), "Sports" (athletes in any sport) or "History, Science, Politics" (essentially a grab bag). Or players can come up with their own category. Just make sure there are a lot of people in the category!

OBJECTIVE:

The ultimate goal for each round is to come up with one famous or known person for every set of initials provided, and for each of a player's famous people to be on the list of at least one other player in the game. That is how players can earn the maximum 100 points.

Player 1 first announces her category and then the ten sets of initials to the group, and everyone writes them down. For example: RD, LB, DT, LD, JL, and so on. These initials represent the first and last names of people that Player 1 was thinking of when she created her list. In this game, the other players don't have to match with Player 1; they simply have to match with at least one other player in the group. For example, in the Entertainment category for the initials LB, there are many possibilities. Players may think of Leonard Bernstein or Linda Blair or Lauren Bacall or Lloyd Bridges. They may even come up with someone who isn't necessarily famous but that they think will be on someone else's list. Anything goes, as long as the name appears on at least one of the other players' lists in the game. If not, they will get negative points for that name. Everyone has five minutes to come up with a match for as many of the ten sets of initials provided as they can, and they can only list *one* person per set of initials. So, if a player thought of the four options above for LB, he must decide on only one of them!

The scoring is key and will determine how many total names out of the ten players want to go for and how much of a risk they are willing to take! A player may only decide to list four, or eight, or somewhere in between, and not put an entry in for all ten. The risks will be outlined in the scoring section.

Players complete their list and turn it over. Once every player is done or the five minutes is up, each player will hand his list to the player next to him. That player will score the list.

SCORING:

One at a time, players will announce who they have on the list in front of them for each set of initials. If nobody else has the same name for a specific set of initials, put an X next to that name on the list. If at least one other person has the name on her list, put a check mark next to that name. For example, if the first initials are RD, you announce the name on your list is Robert De Niro. Two other people say they have Robert De Niro. All three of those players put a check mark next to De Niro. In this game, it doesn't matter how many people had De Niro—as long as at least two people listed it, anyone who had it gets the check mark.

Once names for every set of initials are announced and everyone has check marks or X marks next to every name on their list, it's time to score each list. Multiply the number of check marks by 10 for the positive score. For example, if you have eight check marks, the positive score would be 80. Four check marks = 40. Three check marks = 30. Ten check marks = 100.

Now, add up all the X marks. Multiply the number of X marks by 10 for the negative score. So, for four X marks, the negative score would be -40. Six X marks and the negative score would be -60. Take the positive score and subtract the negative score and you will have the total score for that player. So, if a player has four check marks for 40 positive points and two X marks for 20 negative points, his total score would be 20 for that round. That player decided to only list names for six of the ten initials. Either he couldn't think of names for the other four sets of initials, or he simply didn't want to risk not matching with any of the additional names he came up with. Had he listed three other names and they didn't match, he would have instead had 50 negative points (5 × 10), which would have given him a total score of -10. As you see, there is a steep penalty of -10 points for every name you put down that doesn't match. This is why you may only decide to list names you have a strong feeling about, taking less of a risk. If your list only has seven names on it, your maximum total score potential would be 70, but at least you would end up with positive points if at least four of your seven names matched. On the other hand, you can try to match all ten initial sets and go for 100 points! In this scenario, if you hit six out of ten, your positive score would be 60 (6 × 10) and your negative score would be 40 (4 × 10), giving you a total score of 20. It's up to you to determine the risk for each round, based on the specific category, number of players, the initials provided, and how confident you are in matching at least one person with each of your names.

BONUS POINTS:

You can certainly change the name of this game to 125 if you like and offer a 25-point bonus to any player who risks it all in a round by listing ten and matching all of them! Therefore, a perfect 10 gives you 125 points instead of 100!

ADVANTAGE:

The obvious advantage the player submitting initials has in each round is that she has at least thought of a name to match each set. Still, that player doesn't have to place every name she thought of on her list. She announces her set of initials and decides what kind of risk she is willing to take, like everyone else.

FOR CONSIDERATION:

This is not an easy game. The chances of going 10 for 10 and getting 100 points are slim, especially with few people in the game. However, with fewer than six people, the rules can be altered by allowing players to list two different people for each set of initials. For example, in the entertainment category with the initials MJ, you can submit both "Michael Jackson" and "Mick Jagger." If just one of those people is on someone else's list for MJ, you get the check mark.

Player 2 submits his ten sets of initials for round two.

Important: If a set of initials has already been used in a specific category, you cannot play it again in the same game. Keep the initials which have already been used handy so when it is your turn, you can check your list of initials against those that have already been used.

BIG OR SMALL

WIN BIG BY MATCHING LONGER WORDS WITH MANY PLAYERS

PREPARATION:

Every player thinks of three consecutive letters which are common letters found at the beginning of many words, such as STO, PRO, TEL, PLA, TRA, or STR. Each player comes up with one set of three and waits to introduce it on his turn.

OBJECTIVE:

The goal for each player is to score as many points as possible on each round by matching the other players' answers. The more people who match on a given word, the more points those players receive. In addition, the longer the word, the more points each player receives.

GAME TIME:

Player 1 goes first and announces three letters. For example, let's say Player 1 chooses to use the letters STO, which must be used in that order at the very beginning of all words. Now every player must come up with four words maximum that begin with the letters STO. Three minutes on the clock. The words must be at least four letters, no plurals. Each player wants to match what other players are going to put down. The longer the words and the more people that match the words, the more points received.

SCORING:

For each word a player has on her list, she multiplies the number of people who had the word, including herself, by the number of letters in the word. That is each player's score for that word. For example, let's say there are eight total players in the game with the letters STO for round one. Three players had the word "Stop," which has four letters. Three players × four letters = 12 points for that word. Again, multiply the number of letters in the word by the number of people who matched, and those people who matched earn those points for the word. So, for the three people who matched on "Stop," those three people get 12 points for "Stop." Four players had the word "Story" on their lists. With five letters in that word and four players matching, those four players each get 20 points for "Story." Five players had "Storage" for 35 points each (7 × 5), and two players had "Store" for 10 points each. No points if you are the only one with a word. Therefore, you can go for big words and hope many people have some of those words for a big payday, or be conservative with small words you feel have a better chance of matching. You will still score big with small words if many people have them.

Another Option: You can also change it up and have people list four letters that must be used in your words, but the letters don't have to be in any order. For example, the four letters can be MORP. From these letters, you can spell words such as Prom, Promote, Promotion, Promotional, Promotionally, Romp, Morphine, Metamorphosis, and so on. Same scoring.

NEXT:

Player 2 submits her three letters for round two.

RANK THEM

FIGURE OUT THE MOST OBVIOUS RANKING ORDER IN EACH CATEGORY

PREPARATION:

Each player places five or six famous people (each on a separate card or piece of paper) in a pile and mixes them up with all the others, placing the pile face-down on the table. Next, each player writes four or five categories on separate cards or pieces of paper in another pile, face-down. These categories will be how everyone ranks the famous people. Categories to consider for this game can be anything, such as "Best-Looking," "Richest," "Most Laid-Back," "Most Generous," "Best Hair," "Most Intelligent," "Most Charitable," "Worst-Behaved at School," "Best Athlete," "Tallest," "Most Likely to Live the Longest Life," "Most Likely to Be Leading a Secret Double Life," and so on. Anything goes! Mix each of the two piles up separately.

OBJECTIVE:

This game is all about ranking famous people based on age, intelligence, behavior, wealth, and so on. Think about how most players will rank the three famous people based on the category selected. Score the most points by succeeding in coming up with the most popular ranking order in each round.

Player 1 randomly selects four famous people from the first pile and then she picks up one card from the category pile. She then makes the decision to throw one of the four famous people out. She doesn't have to say which one. This is all based on how competitive she wants to make the ranking. She may also feel that one of the people simply may not belong in this category, or won't make it as much fun as the others. She must choose three from the four, though, and can't start picking out other cards. Player 1 then announces the three famous people and the category to the group, and everyone must now rank them according to the category chosen from first to third. So, for the category "Most Wealthy," 1 is Most Wealthy and 3 is Least Wealthy of the three. No talking once the famous people are announced. Players have thirty seconds to make their ranking, then turn their paper over. Players want to match other people with the same exact order for points. Keep in mind that the actual answer (even if there is one) does not matter in this game! The only ranking order that matters is the one everyone puts down. That is the only way players can score.

SCORING:

Once everyone has turned over their paper, scoring commences. Player 1 reads her rank order first. For every player who has the same order as Player 1, multiply the number of people who have that order by itself. That is the number of points each person gets. Same goes for every other combination. So, for the "Most Wealthy" category with Brad Pitt,

Jennifer Lopez, and Adam Sandler, if three people had Pitt, Lopez, and Sandler in that order, those three would get 9 points. If two people had Lopez, Sandler, and Pitt, those two would get 4 points, and if one person had Sandler, Pitt, and Lopez in that order, that one person gets 1 point for being unique.

NEXT:

Then Player 2 picks another category from the category pile and four famous people from that pile, tosses out one, and announces the three selected for round two rankings.

ASSOCIATION

4+ PLAYERS

FIGURE OUT WHO SAID WHAT TO KEEP PACE

PREPARATION:

Each player thinks of one person, one place, and one thing, and writes each of them on separate pieces of paper or index cards. The three items from each player get mixed up all together and placed in a pile face-down on the table or in a hat.

> **Important:** Your person must be someone who is known to the group, such as Julia Roberts or Albert Einstein, or it can be someone who isn't necessarily famous but who everyone in your particular group knows. The place must be a place everyone knows, such as a city, state, country, or even Disney World. The thing can be anything, just as long as everyone in your group knows what that thing is.

Next, someone is assigned to place all of the letters of the alphabet on separate small pieces of paper in another pile or hat, mixed up.

Match one or both of your partners when it is your turn to match. Figure out exactly who said what when others are try-ing to match.

Play begins with Players 1, 2, and 3 trying to match their an-swers while the others wait to figure out who said what once the answers are revealed. Here is how it works: Player 1 first picks out four random letters from the hat. He reads them out loud so everyone can write them down. He then picks out one random person, place, or thing from that pile. He announces what he selected. Sixty seconds are then put on the clock and each of the three players (in this case, Players 1, 2, and 3) must now think of one word that is most associated with that person, place, or thing, and that he or she thinks the other two would also put down. However, the one word put down *must* begin with one of the four chosen letters!

For example, let's say the four letters picked out of the pile were A, G, P, and W. Then from the person, place, or thing pile Player 1 randomly selected "Las Vegas." Players 1, 2, and 3 now had to each think of *one* word that would most be as-sociated with Las Vegas that begins with either A, G, P, or W.

There can be no communication among any of the players during the sixty seconds, and no looking at anyone's paper. Once the sixty seconds are up, pens go down and Player 1 collects the answers from Players 2 and 3 without showing anyone else in the game who wrote what.

First, Player 1 must see if any of the three of them matched. If nobody matched, then Player 1 reads out loud the three different words selected from the three players in random order to everyone else in the game, without revealing who wrote which word. If Player 1 sees that two players matched, he says out loud the two words that were submitted, without revealing which one was the match. (In other words, if the words submitted for the example were "Gambling," "Gambling," and "Winning," Player 1 would only say, "Gambling and Winning." The other players have to guess which word was said twice.) In either case, the other players in the game now take thirty seconds to write down who they thought had each word.

However, if all three of them matched, Player 1 does not say the matching word they all put down! The rest of the group now has thirty seconds to figure out what that word is and writes that word on a piece of paper.

SCORING FOR PLAYERS TRYING TO MATCH IN EACH ROUND:

Players 1, 2, and 3 receive 20 points each if they all match. If two of the three players match, those two players each receive 10 points and the other player receives nothing. If there is no match among the three players, they each receive nothing for that round.

SCORING FOR PLAYERS TRYING TO GUESS WHO SAID WHAT IN EACH ROUND:

If there was no match among the three players and you were successful in determining who said what, you receive 5 points. (You must get them all right!) If two of the players matched and you were successful in guessing who submitted which word, and which one matched, you receive 10 points (The same amount that those two players received). If all three of the players matched and you were successful in coming up with the word they all put down, you receive 20 points (The same amount that those three players received).

In the example above with Las Vegas and the letters A, G, P, and W, there could be several possible answers, such as "Win," "Party," or "Gamble." If all three said "Gamble," that's 20 points for those players and only the players who guessed the word was "Gamble" would also receive the 20 points.

Obviously, in the Las Vegas case with those letters there were some solid options. You may not get that lucky, however. In several cases, it will be really difficult to find a match based on the random letters selected.

IMPORTANT RULE:

Any form of the word qualifies as a match. Gamble, Gambling, Gambler, and so on all count as a match.

NEXT:

Players 2, 3, and 4 try to match while the rest of the players guess. Then 3, 4, and 5, and so on until each player has had three chances to match with two other partners.

PERCENTAGES

3+ PLAYERS

HOW ACCURATE ARE YOUR PERCENTAGE ESTIMATES?

PREPARATION:

Each player thinks of a percentage question to pose to the group, such as: "What percentage of people in this restaurant were born in the United States?"

"What percentage of last weekend did Jerry spend sleeping?"

"What percentage of all plastic surgeries are performed on people over fifty?" When coming up with the question, the actual answer is irrelevant—it's all about what the other players *think* the answer is!

OBJECTIVE:

Be as close as possible to the majority opinion for each question to earn maximum points.

GAME TIME:

Player 1 poses her question first. Let's say that question is, "What percentage of people in this restaurant were born in the United States?" Each player now only has 11 options, from 0 to 100 by 10. In other words, the answer can only be 0, 10, 20, 30, 40, and so on, all the way to 100. Players write down their guess on a piece of paper without sharing with anyone, and then turn over their paper. No talking after the question is announced!

SCORING:

Players want to have the most common answer for each round of the game. For each question, every player starts with 30 points. If a player has the most common answer, she keeps her 30 points. Otherwise, she subtracts the number of percentage points she is away from the common answer from 30 for her score that round. Therefore, if the common percentage answer was 40 and you had 20, your score for that round would be 10. You were 20 from the common answer, and 30 - 20 = 10. Everyone who said 40 would keep the starting 30 points.

In Case of a Tie:

For example, if three people in your group of eight said 60 and three people said 40, then all of those people with 60 and 40 keep their 30 points. The two people who were off take the closest winning percentage to their answer and subtract the difference from there. For example, if one person said 30, then he would subtract 10 from the 30 since he was 10 points off from the 40 answer. His score for that round would be 20. If another player said 80, then he would subtract 20 from 30 since he was 20 off from the 60 answer. His score would be 10. If you are 30 points or more from the common answer, you get 0 points for that question. No negative points in this game. Finally, if everyone has a different answer to a question, no points are awarded for that round.

NEXT:

Player 2 poses his question to the group and everyone writes down their percentage answer.

IT'S A NUMBERS GAME

PREPARATION:

Each player comes up with a question that requires the answer to be a specific number. The players don't have to know the actual answer to the question. For example, one question might be, "How many shows are playing on Broadway this month?" Another question might be, "How many major universities are there in the state of Wyoming?" Another could be, "How many number-one hits did Michael Jackson produce?" Or, "How many people in this restaurant will end up ordering the lobster special tonight?" Once all players have their question requiring a specific number answer, they now have to come up with four possible answers from which every player in the game will choose. The only rule is that the choices cannot be within 1 of each other. For example, the choices cannot be 1, 2, 3, or 4, but they could be 1, 3, 5, and 7. They could also be 100, 200, 350, and 3,000. It all depends on the question itself.

For each round, players match their answer with a lot of the other players to earn the maximum points in each round. When asking a question, make sure at least one player's answer is off from the rest of the group—and that one person should not be the one asking the question!

GAME TIME:

Player 1 poses his question to the group, along with the four possible answers he came up with. Then each player (including Player 1) takes thirty seconds to make her selection and writes it down on a piece of paper without letting anyone see her answer, and places it face-down on the table. Nobody should be giving any hints as to what number she is going to select! Players want to take an educated guess as to what they think everyone else will pick. They are simply trying to match the answer of the majority of the players in the game for maximum points.

SCORING:

Example: Player 1 posed the question, "How many people in this restaurant will end up ordering the lobster special tonight?" He then provided four possible answers: 4, 14, 21, and 55. Player 1 then asks the group who had each number option one at a time. Multiply the number of people who chose the same answer by itself for the point total for those people. If four people said 21, those four people each get 16 points. If two people had 55, those two people each get 4 points. If one person had 14, that person gets one point for being unique. However, if there are 6 people in the game and everyone chose the same number, all of those people get 36 points—with one major exception: The player who came up with the question and the answer choices gets no points at all! Therefore, when coming up with the possible number answers to your question, don't make it too easy! If you do, you risk getting nothing while everyone else scores big! You merely want to offer options that won't have an overly obvious top choice—ideally, you want one person to select a different answer than everyone else and you want *your* answer to be in the majority

NEXT:

Player 2 poses her question and four number options to the group, and play continues.

I hese games are all about discovering a whole bunch of things you never knew about the people in your group. How well do you truly know members of your own family and your best friends? The revelations can often be intriguing, fun, eye-popping, bizarre, and sometimes downright hilarious. Playing with people you know well will test how well you truly know them. Playing with strangers could lead to quickly forming new bonds and relationships. Either way, you'll most likely remember less about who won the games and much more about everyone's past, present, future, dreams, hobbies, and interests.

MY FAVORITE THINGS

HOW WELL DO YOU KNOW THE INTERESTS OF THE PLAYERS IN YOUR GROUP?

PREPARATION:

Each player comes up with five activities that people like to do—any activities, from cooking, to working out, playing cards, watching TV, surfing, gardening, playing billiards, and so on. (Or pull from the sample list for ideas.) Write each activity down on a separate piece of paper and place them all in a hat or face-down on a table mixed in with all of the others.

OBJECTIVE:

To match the rank order of the player who provides the answer as best as you can in every round.

GAME TIME:

Player 1 goes first and pulls five random activities from the pile. Player 1 announces them to the group and everyone writes them down. Player 1 must now rank them in order from what she would consider to be her most favorite to her least favorite. Player 1 must be honest about which activities would be most desirable and least desirable out of the five she selected. Every other player must now also place the selected items in the order of how they think Player 1 will list them. This is all about Player 1 and her interest in the selected activities—nothing to do with how you would rank them yourself if it were about you.

Player 1 writes her list and does not speak or do anything to hint about the order. Once Player 1 has her list and every other player has their rank order for Player 1, players reveal what they think the correct order is and points are awarded. One at a time, players go around the table revealing their order and reasoning why they think Player 1 placed each item first, second, third, fourth, or fifth. Players don't have to give their reasoning, but that tends to be a lot of fun based on how well they know (or think they know) Player 1. Player 1 does not comment when these lists are being read. Finally, Player 1 reveals the correct order and why, and points are tallied.

SCORING:

For the players trying to get the order right from Player 1, points are tallied in the following way:

- First position correct: 10 points
- Second position correct: 8 points
- Third position correct: 6 points
- Fourth position correct: 4 points
- Fifth position correct: 2 points
- 10 bonus points if you get them all right!

Total possible points for a player guessing are 40 points. (10 + 8 + 6 + 4 + 2 plus 10 bonus points.) For Player 1, she receives 3 points for every correct match. In other words, if Player 2 matched two positions correctly, Player 1 gets 6 points for Player 2's scorecard, regardless of which positions were correct. If Player 3 matched three positions correctly, Player 1 gets 9 points for Player 3's scorecard, and so on.

NEXT:

Player 2 now randomly picks five activities out of the pile and announces them. Player 2 ranks them from most favorite to least and everyone tries to figure out his order, and so on.

FAVORITE THINGS IDEAS:

Stumped and need help coming up with ideas for this game? Check out this sample list. We've included some normal activities, some off-the-wall activities, and some activities that most people wouldn't enjoy at all! It can be fun to include a variety to make the game more interesting.

Snow tubing

Weight lifting

Playing poker

Singing karaoke

Painting

Mud wrestling

Pillow fighting

Shaving someone's back

Eating grapes

Going to a petting zoo

Giving a toast at a wedding

Riding a roller coaster

Playing backgammon

Jumping on a trampoline

Eating oysters

Sunbathing

Playing chess

Attending the opera

Watching a golf tournament on TV

Playing with kittens

Reading a book about insects

Baking

Throwing a pineapple back and forth to a friend. First one to drop it loses.

Taking a bath

Square dancing

Playing ping pong

Eating Froot Loops

Getting a massage

Waiting in a two-hour
line to get tickets for a
Broadway show

Playing guitar in a rock band

Soaking in a hot tub

Playing Bingo

Playing Frisbee

Playing "pin the tail on the
donkey"

Reading a romance novel

Camping

Gardening

Doing yoga

Climbing a rock wall

Attending a ballet

Taking ballroom dancing
classes

Spending a week in Paris

Spending two weeks in
Boise, Idaho

Playing hide-and-seek

Eating a banana

Snorkeling

Listening to Mozart

Playing billiards

Fishing

Watching NASCAR

Eating cheesecake

Spending a week at
Disney World

Cleaning your house

Being tickled for thirty
seconds

Skateboarding

Horseback riding

Going on a cruise

Building a sandcastle

Eating pumpkin pie

Going to the circus

Getting a tattoo

Going to the dentist

Playing baseball

Eating bagels and cream
cheese

Hanging out at the airport

Playing musical chairs

Watching the weather
channel

Putting together IKEA
furniture

Eating Italian food

Knitting a sweater

Sleeping in a tent for a week

Playing a video game

Milking a cow

Running a marathon

Getting licked in the face
by an elephant

Eating Jell-O

Playing with a dog

Watching a soccer match

Playing basketball

Performing surgery

Shoveling snow

Eating chocolate-
covered ants

Watching a Western

Building a tree house

Doing laundry

Starring in a one-person
show on Broadway

Eating pickles

Playing soccer

Laying in the sun

Reading the Sunday paper

Going to a comedy club

Going to a monster
truck rally

Eating McDonald's

Playing Monopoly

Getting punched in the leg

Walking into a spider web
with three spiders on it

Watching the fishing channel
for two hours

Playing bridge

Getting into a fight with a
baboon

Working for the FBI

HOW MANY TIMES?

4+
PLAYERS

///

HOW WELL DO YOU KNOW THE HISTORY OF THE PLAYERS IN YOUR GROUP?

PREPARATION:

Each player comes up with a question that begins with "How many . . . ?" such as, "How many times have you been bitten by a mosquito in your life?" or "How many times have you been to the beach in your life?" or "How many times have you flown on an airplane?" or "How many total countries have you been to in your life?" or "How many total music concerts have you been to in your life?" Any question will work if it will lead to a bunch of different answers that are all numbers. Questions just can't get so specific that everyone's answer is relatively the same. Players can either write down their questions or just remember them for their turn.

OBJECTIVE:

To match each number provided with the player who submitted it on each question for maximum points.

GAME TIME:

Player 1 begins by asking the group his question about how many times everyone in the group has done something specific in their lives. For this example, let's say Player 1 asks, "How many times have you thrown up in your life?" The group must agree that the question is valid and will produce a variety of answers. Everyone writes down their answer on a small piece of paper (omitting their name) and places it in the center of the table. Players must give a specific number that is their honest guess as to how many, even if they have no clue about the exact number. They can't just say "over 100" or "less than 50." Mix all the numbers up and then each player picks one out of the pile. One at a time, each player reads the number he picked out and everyone writes it down and makes a list. Once all of the numbers are written down, each player assigns a number to each player in the game based on an educated guess. Once everyone is done assigning a number to a player and has his complete list, the answers are revealed.

SCORING:

You earn 5 points for every correct match and a bonus 50 points if you get them all right.

> **Note:** If there are more than eight players in the game, split the group into two for each activity to make it easier to match answers. So, if you have ten players, the first five people will write number answers to the question and everyone will try to match those five, instead of the more difficult task of matching numbers with ten or more players. Then, the next five players will write their numbers for the same question and everyone will try to match those.

NEXT:

Player 2 now asks her question, and so on.

BUCKET LIST

3+
PLAYERS

HOW WELL DO YOU KNOW THE DREAMS OF THE PLAYERS IN YOUR GROUP?

PREPARATION:

Each player thinks of three bucket list items. These are things they haven't accomplished in their life but definitely want to do at some point. For example, common bucket list items for people might be: Sky Diving, South African Safari, See the Northern Lights, Run a Marathon, See the Great Wall of China, Learn to Play an Instrument, and so on. Players write down three items that are definitely on their list. Now each player also must come up with three bucket list items that are *not* on their list, but could definitely be on the lists of many other people. In the end, every player has a list of six bucket list items, three that are real items and three that are not.

Note: You don't want every one of your real bucket list items to be very obvious, and you want the three fake items to be thought of as a real potential for you when they are actually things you have no true desire to do. You must, however, be honest about your items.

To figure out which three items are the *real* bucket list items for each player in the game for maximum points.

Player 1 goes first and announces her six bucket list items in no particular order. Every other player writes them down and now has to figure out which are the three *real* bucket list items of Player 1. No talking after Player 1 announces her items; two minutes on the clock. Each player writes what he thinks are the three real items for Player 1 on a card or piece of paper and places it face-down in front of him. Player 1 now circles her three true bucket list items on her card or paper and places it face-down in front of her. Each player (except Player 1) now passes his card to the player to his right with his name on it so that player can read his answers and score his card. Skip Player 1 in this process. Each player will now read the guesses of the player whose card they have. Player 1 will not comment. Once all cards have been read, Player 1 will reveal her answers.

Figure out all three bucket list items and you get 50 points. Two items gets you 25 points. One item gets you 5 points. If you get them all wrong, you lose 25 points! (The player who created the list gets no points in this game.)

Player 2 announces his six bucket list items, and round two begins.

WHICH IS TRUE?

4–10
PLAYERS

//

SOME THINGS ABOUT YOU CAN BE A BIG SURPRISE

PREPARATION:

Each player thinks of four things people don't know about them, then writes each statement about themselves down on a separate index card in the third person. For example, Brian would write something like, "Brian was bitten by a monkey when he was six years old," or, "Brian has never eaten a hot dog in his life," or, "Brian has never seen *Star Wars*." They must all be true statements written in the third person, each written on a separate card.

> **Important:** The ideal scenario is for nobody to know these things about you. However, in some situations with spouses or siblings, it may be difficult to fool everyone. Do your best. Just know that if someone knows the truth about one of your statements, that person will have an advantage in the game.

Once players have their four true statements, now they must also think of four false statements. These are also written in the third person, but these statements are definitely false. However, it is important to make them believable! The goal is to make people think that any of these false statements could actually be true. Keep the four true statements separate from the four false statements. Now place all of the true statements face-down on the table with everyone else's true statements. Player 1 mixes them all very well, without looking at them, and collects them in a separate pile and places them on the table in front of him to the left. Now everyone places their false statements on the table and Player 1 mixes those together without looking at them and puts that mixed-up pile in front of him on the right.

OBJECTIVE:

To figure out which of the two items selected is true each time for maximum points.

GAME TIME:

Player 1 begins and picks up one card from the true pile and one from the false pile without looking at them. He mixes them face-down on the table so that there is no way he can now know which is true and which is false. He picks them both up and turns them over. He gives each one a number and announces them both to the other players. For example, he may say, "Number one: Brian only bathes once a week," and "Number two: Rebecca used to have an imaginary friend named Hopscotch." One of these statements is true, and everyone (except for Brian and Rebecca) will have to guess, including Player 1. Players are given fifteen seconds or so to think about it. Then, at the count of three, all players will put up one or two fingers to show which one they are voting for as the true statement. Scores are then tallied. Keep in mind that from time to time, both statements may be about the same person, since the piles were mixed and they are chosen randomly. That's perfectly fine. That person will be the only one not guessing for those two options. However, any time that happens, that person may not vote the next time his name doesn't appear on either statement. This rule is in place to ensure that everyone in the game gets to guess an equal number of times and has the same total score potential. With the last two true and false statements left, if the same person is on both of those statements, that person's guess the last time he didn't show up on either card won't count.

Once guesses are revealed, the players whose statements were given reveal which was true. Player 1 then writes the word "true" on the card with the true statement, along with the names of the players who got it right. Player 1 writes the word "false" on the card with the false statement, along with the names of the players who got it wrong. Player 1 places those two cards in a separate pile. Then Player 1 draws two more cards from each of the piles, mixes them thoroughly, and then reads them out loud, repeating the process and finishing by writing the names of the players who got it right on the True card and those who got it wrong on the False card. Then, Player 1 places those cards in the pile he started with all of the answers.

SCORING:

Once all of the cards have been read and guesses made, there will be one pile of cards with names on them. Player 1 reads the names on all the true and false cards and everyone builds their scores. If Player 1 reads your name on a true statement card, you get 5 points. However, if Player 1 reads your name on a false card statement, the player who submitted that statement gets 10 points for fooling you. So for example, if the statement "John eats Pizza at least three times a week" is false and three people thought it was true,

John would get 30 points for fooling three people. Again, for every one of the false statements *you* submitted, you get 10 points per person you fooled.

So for John, if his name was on seven true statement cards, that means he got seven right and he gets 35 points. For John's false statements, if he fooled two people on one statement, three people on another statement, one person on another statement, and nobody on his fourth statement, he would add another 60 points (10 × 6). John's total score = 95.

Important: No taking notes during the game. The only writing anyone can do once the game begins is to record who got each statement right or wrong once the correct answer is revealed. This rule is in place to prevent anyone from keeping track of how many true or false statements have been made by each person.

Note: You can also rotate who mixes and reads each round of true and false cards and records the answers. Just make sure while you are passing the piles that you never mix the true and false piles together.

MY FAVORITE YEAR

4–8
PLAYERS

WHICH OF THESE EVENTS REALLY HAPPENED?

PREPARATION:

Each player thinks of three different events that happened to them at specific years in their life. Players write down each event and the associated year in the third person, making sure nobody in the game is aware that these events took place. In fact, there should be no hints in the story that would lead anyone to believe that player definitely wrote it. For example, Laura must write something like, "In 2012, Laura went on a safari and a deer crashed into her tour bus," or, "In 1995, Laura ate octopus for the first time." If the year is slightly off, that's OK. Just make sure each event is absolutely true and it happened either in that year or very close to it. Each event should be written on a separate card legibly, so anyone will be able to read it. Now, each player thinks of a made-up event that never happened to them but sounds completely believable. Write this event in the third person like the other three. Now players have four events written about themselves on four separate cards. Finally, each player makes up one event for the person to their left and one event for the person to their right. For example, if Jennifer is sitting to Laura's right and Bill is sitting to Laura's left, then Laura must now make up one event for Jennifer and one event for Bill. She also writes them in the third person, as if Bill and Jennifer had written the events themselves. For example, Laura may write, "In 2014, Jennifer witnessed a car crash on the highway, stopped to call 911, and waited with the victims for the ambulance." This story must be completely made-up but should be believable, so people will have a tough time deciding if it is true. Again, Laura will write one story for Jennifer and one story for Bill. Every player will do the same; one story for the player to the left and one story for the player to the right. So, in the end each player will have created six events, three that are true, one they made up about themselves, and two they made up for other people in the game. This way, half of the stories in the game are true and half are false. Everyone submits their six events to a pile in the middle of the table or in a hat and they are all mixed up.

OBJECTIVE:

To figure out which events are true and which events are completely made-up.

GAME TIME:

Player 1 begins by picking one random event from the hat and reading it. Each player now takes fifteen seconds to determine if the event is true or false. At the count of three, every player holds up their T or F card. The answer is revealed and points are awarded.

Important: Any time an event is picked out, the player who is the subject of the event will not have a guess for the event. In addition, the author of a false event will obviously not guess for that event either. However, the author of a false event *will not reveal this information* and will pretend to guess anyway! You do not want others to figure out that this was a made-up event and give those players an easy point!

Then, Player 2 picks the next event from the hat and reads it, and the process continues. Again, players don't vote when the event is about them. Players *do* vote for a false event they made up about someone else, without giving away that they wrote it, but that vote won't be tallied. Keep rotating around the table, giving each player a chance to select events from the hat one at a time.

Note: The obvious advantage anyone has in this game is when you pick a card from the hat, you may recognize the handwriting of someone who wrote an event about someone else. Therefore, when writing all of your events, true or false, you may want to use different handwriting—as long as you keep them all legible!

SCORING:

Each player receives one point per correct guess. Answers are revealed immediately after the guesses are revealed. Each player will have six events where they do not vote. Therefore, with a total of five players in the game and thirty total events, each player will have the chance to achieve a maximum of 24 points.

Important: No taking notes during the game. It is up to you to try to remember how many true or false statements have been announced for each player. You can then try to calculate your odds of getting the answer correct, if that is part of your strategy.

LUNCH WITH MY ROLE MODEL

3+ PLAYERS

//

FIGURE OUT EVERYONE'S FAVORITE LUNCH GUESTS

PREPARATION:

Each player writes down the names of five or six famous people, then mixes them up with all the others and places the pile in a hat or face-down on the table. These famous people should be people you would love to invite to lunch, just the two of you for a one-hour conversation. They can be dead or alive, although if you were to have lunch with them it would naturally be the living version.

OBJECTIVE:

Try to match the exact order of the player whose turn it is to determine who she would prefer to have lunch with the most, then second, and then last from the three that were randomly selected.

Player 1 goes first and selects four random famous people from the pile, then puts one of them back. The one she puts back is completely up to her. It doesn't matter if any of these are people Player 1 submitted herself or not. The purpose of submitting people is so that at least one person in the group has the strong desire to have lunch with every famous person in the pile. Player 1 announces the three people she selected and everyone writes them down. Player 1 now determines her order, from most interested to have lunch with at number one to least interested at number three. Player 1 *must be honest* about her order. She is not trying to fool the other players—in fact, she only gets points if the other players guess correctly! (More on that in "Scoring.") Player 1 must also be completely silent and not give any hints to anyone about what her ranking order will be.

Every other player tries to figure out what Player 1's order will be, and each player makes their list for Player 1. For example, if the three people selected were Oprah, John Lennon, and JFK, Player 1 might have this order: John Lennon, JFK, Oprah. Or, Oprah, John Lennon, JFK. There are several possibilities, of course. Every other player has his guess written down as to what he thinks Player 1's order would be. Once all lists are finished, pens go down. Player 2 goes first and announces what his list is for Player 1. Part of the fun of this game is the reasoning players give for why they think the player would rank them a certain way. In this case, Player 2 can explain his guess and why he thinks he matched with Player 1. Everyone goes around the room revealing his guess and explaining why, if he desires. Players don't have to give a reason and can simply say their order, but explaining why they have what they have is definitely part of the fun. Player 1 should just listen to everyone's stories as to why they think they know her order without responding or giving anything away. Once the last person provides his guess, Player 1 reveals her true order and why, and points are then tallied.

SCORING:

Two points are awarded for every player who has the same order as Player 1. You can only score if you have the exact order.

Player 1 can only score if *everyone else* matches her order exactly! If that happens, Player 1 receives points equivalent to the total number of players in the game. So, with seven total players, if all six match the exact order of Player 1, Player 1 receives 7 points. If just one person is off, Player 1 gets no points for her round.

> **Important:** Again, when it is your turn to pick the three famous people and have everyone try to match you, you cannot give any hints as to how you are going to rank them. You must be completely silent, write them down without letting anyone see, and turn your card over until everyone else is done making their guesses.

NEXT:

Player 2 selects four random famous people from the hat, discards one of them, and the game continues with everyone trying to figure out Player 2's order . . . and so on.

NOT IN A MILLION YEARS

//

ANYTHING IS POSSIBLE!

PREPARATION:

Each player comes up with five things that he is pretty certain he will never do or say for the rest of his life. These are things that I call one-percenters. In other words, there is a one-percent chance I will ever eat monkey brains. Or, there is a one-percent chance I will ever jump out of a plane. Or, there is a one-percent chance I will ever say a specific word out loud. The things put on the list must be actual things that at least some people in the world actually do, but the player chooses not to do them. It doesn't have to be that a lot of people do or say these things, but they do have to be things that are actually possible and could be done if wanted. No fantasies! For example, players can't say something like, "See a hobbit" or "Play with a Dinosaur." It must be something that could actually be done today or at some time this year if given the chance, but the chances that it will ever happen are extremely slim, because the player would choose not to do it.

OBJECTIVE:

To accurately guess how each player would rank the chances of doing things they would never really do from most likely to least likely.

GAME TIME:

Player 1 goes first and shares his list of five one-percenters. If one of the things is something he would never say, he can merely show it to everyone on the paper so that he doesn't have to say it. Once every player writes them down, Player 1 begins ranking his list of five in the order he would potentially actually do them, even though the chances are extremely slim. His number one is the one he would most likely say or do. Number five is least likely. The others fall in rank accordingly. Player 1 must come up with a clear explanation for why he has ranked them the way he has when he reveals his answers. That's the truly fun part of this game—listening to the player make a case for why he would potentially do each one over the other, even though they are farthest from any of his true interests or desires. Every other player must try to figure out what Player 1's exact ranking will be. The other players write their orders down without letting anyone see. Once Player 1 is done and all guesses are written down, Player 1 reveals his answers from least likely to most likely, five to one. As he moves up his list from five to one, he should explain why he decided he would do the next thing more than the thing or things that came before it. For example, for his third ranked thing, he must explain why there's a better chance he would do that over the thing he listed in the number four position and the thing he listed in the number five position.

For the players trying to get the order right from Player 1, points are tallied in the following way:

- First position correct: 10 points
- Second position correct: 8 points
- Third position correct: 6 points
- Fourth position correct: 4 points
- Fifth position correct: 2 points
- 10 bonus points if you get them all right!

Total possible points for a player guessing are 40 points (10 + 8 + 6 + 4 + 2 plus 10 bonus points). Player 1 receives 3 points for every correct match. In other words, if Player 2 matched two positions correctly, Player 1 gets 6 points for Player 2's scorecard, regardless of which positions were correct. If Player 3 matched three positions correctly, Player 1 gets 9 points for Player 3's scorecard, and so on.

NEXT:

Player 2 now shares her list of five things she would most likely never do, and the game continues.

CHOICES

4+ PLAYERS   OPTIONAL

//

FUN TIMES WITH DIFFICULT OPTIONS

PREPARATION:

None.

OBJECTIVE:

Create a difficult choice for the player to your right, one that will lead to a split decision from the rest of the group!

GAME TIME:

Player 1 announces a very difficult choice between two options for Player 2. Peanuts or pretzels? Shakira or Mariah Carey? Walking on hot coals for two minutes or lying on a bed of nails for two hours? Those examples may not be difficult choices for certain players in your group. However, it's all about the person sitting to your right. What would be a difficult choice for that person? In this case, it's all about Player 2 (sitting to the right of Player 1). Once Player 1 announces the two options out loud, Player 2 must either whisper to Player 1 or show one or two fingers under the table indicating her choice. Player 2 must give an honest answer. At the count of three, all of the other players reveal their guesses as to what Player 2 chose. There can be no talking or discussing among the group after Player 1 announces the choices up until the players reveal their guesses. Player 2 reveals her answer and points are then given out.

SCORING:

Two points to every player who guesses the right answer.

The player coming up with the choices (Player 1 in this example) gets 5 points if the votes for each option were split evenly among the group. With an even number of players guessing in the game, the votes must be 2–2, 3–3, 4–4, and so on for Player 1 to get the 5 points. With an odd number of players guessing in the game, the votes must be uneven by only 1, such as 2–1, 3–2, and so on. No points for Player 1 if the voting is uneven by more than 1 (4–2, 3–1, 5–0, and so on). Therefore, the object when coming up with the options for the player next to you is to provide a very difficult choice that will not lead to an easy or obvious decision for both the player choosing and the guessers. The one who chooses (Player 2 in this case) does not get points for her turn.

> **Important:** Player 2 must be honest when providing her answer and cannot lead anyone on or give any hints to the group as to which option she has chosen before anyone guesses. Also, there should be no discussion whatsoever once the choices are offered up and until the guesses are made.

NEXT:

Play continues with Player 2 giving a difficult choice between two items for Player 3, and so on. Once you get back to Player 1, you can rotate by going to the left this time. For example, with six players in the game, after Player 6 gives two choices to Player 1, Player 1 can now go the other way and give two choices to Player 6. Player 6 would then give choices to Player 5, and so on.

CAREERS

3+ PLAYERS   OPTIONAL

///

> IF YOU COULD CHANGE YOUR
> JOB FOR JUST ONE DAY, WHAT
> WOULD YOU DO?

PREPARATION:

Each player comes up with five occupations that they are pretty sure nobody in the game currently has. Any occupation, such as therapist, taxi driver, diplomat, professional wrestler, talk show host, auto mechanic, comedian, astronaut, public bathroom attendant, or even President of the United States will do. Anything goes. Players place their five occupations, each on a separate paper or index card, in a hat or mixed-up pile on the table.

OBJECTIVE:

To figure out the level of interest each player has in performing the job he randomly picks each time.

GAME TIME:

Player 1 goes first and picks a random occupation from the hat and announces it to the group, without giving any indication as to his level of interest in the occupation. Player 1 must then determine just how interested he would be in doing that job if he had the opportunity and was pretty good at it. He has four different numbers he can write on his paper (without letting anyone see) and he must be completely honest about his answer. The numbers are:

1. You have no interest in performing the job whatsoever! Not even for one day.
2. You are slightly curious and would definitely try the job out for a day or two, or even as much as a week.
3. You would definitely be interested in doing this job for at least a few months and perhaps as much as six months, but that would probably be enough, and you would have no interest in making this a new career.
4. This is one of your dream jobs and you would love to do it for at least a year or two, and perhaps even as a career.

While Player 1 is determining his answer, every other player in the game has to figure out what Player 1 will say and write that number down on a piece of paper. Once everyone is done, the answer is revealed and points are awarded to the guessers.

SCORING:

The player who draws the occupation from the pile in each round does not score. He must simply give an honest answer about his level of interest: 1, 2, 3, or 4.

The guessers win 2 points if they match the player on the nose. You win no points if you are off by 1 (for example, Player 1 says 3 and you say 2). You lose 2 points if you are off by 2 (for example, Player 1 says 3 and you say 1). Finally, you lose 5 points if you are off by 3 (For example, Player 1 says 4 and you say 1, or vice versa).

NEXT:

Player 2 now draws from the pile, and so on.

WHAT YOU DIDN'T KNOW ABOUT BOB

4+ PLAYERS

> ### SURPRISE YOUR FRIENDS, AND BE THE BEST AT FIGURING OUT THEIR SURPRISES!

PREPARATION:

For each round of this game, players must come up with one surprise item about themselves in each of two categories: 1) I'm a Fan; 2) I'm Not a Fan.

Here are some examples of what to place in each category:

I'm a Fan

For this category, list anything you like, such as a specific movie, TV show, actor, athlete, food, place, or activity. Activities might include yoga, going to the opera, dancing, going to the beach, cycling, going to the movies, riding roller coasters, eating cereal with orange juice instead of milk, and so on. (For example, you may be playing with a group of people who know many of your favorite things, such as a favorite sports team, or movie, or vacation spot, or that you love eating spaghetti and running marathons. But do they know *everything* you like? Probably not! Perhaps there's a TV show you secretly enjoy, or a food you used to eat and loved as a kid. Or maybe there's a silly activity you really enjoy doing but don't talk about, or an actor or actress you find intriguing. You should be able to find some fun surprises in the "I'm a Fan" category.)

I'm Not a Fan

For this category, list something specific you either don't like *or* have never experienced. In other words, it doesn't necessarily have to be something or someone you don't like. It can simply be something you have never tried, a place you have never visited, or something you have never seen such as a movie, show, event, and so on. (For example, perhaps you're a world traveler and everyone knows it, but there's a city everyone thinks you probably visited that you haven't. Or maybe everyone is under the impression you couldn't possibly be afraid of anything, but panda bears absolutely freak you out.)

Each player writes her "I'm a Fan" item on a small piece of paper without letting anyone see and places her name under the item. It should simply read something like this: "Riding on the back of a motorcycle," and underneath that sentence the player's name. Each player then folds the piece of paper several times and throws it in a hat with everyone else's papers. Players do the same with their "Not a Fan" items, placing those in a separate pile or hat. There should now be two piles of hats with all of the "I'm a Fan" items mixed together in one pile, and the "I'm Not a Fan" items in another pile.

OBJECTIVE:

Players must attempt to surprise the other players by coming up with things they didn't know that player liked or disliked/never experienced. The biggest surprises usually score the most points.

There are two rounds of this game. Place the "I'm Not a Fan" pile aside for the time being. It will be used in the second round. One at a time, each player picks out a random piece from the "I'm a Fan" pile and looks at it without letting anyone see what she picked. Players may end up picking their own piece, and that's perfectly fine (though it puts them at a slight disadvantage).

Next, every player makes three columns on another piece of paper. The first column is for the list of "I'm a Fan" items. The second column should be titled *My Guesses* and is for players to fill in which player they feel is a match with each item listed. The third column, titled *Correct Answers*, is for the correct person once the answers are revealed. Then players add rows equal to the number of players, making a chart. (For example, if you have six players in the game, make six rows and number them from 1 to 6 down the side for the first column.)

Player 1 begins and reads aloud the item he selected from the hat, without revealing the person who wrote that item. Every player now has to place that item next to the number 1 on the list in the far left "I'm a Fan" column. Player 2 now reads the item she selected, and everyone places that item next to number 2 in the "I'm a Fan" column. Player 3 then reads his item, and so on. Once all of the items are read, everyone guesses which item belongs to which player and writes each player's name in column two next to the appropriate item.

Note: Obviously, you know your own, and if you didn't pick your own "I'm a Fan" item out of the hat, then you know who matches up with two of the items and you just have to figure out the rest.

Once everyone is done filling out column two, the true matches are revealed for each item, beginning with the first item on the list. Players simply announce that the item is theirs when it is read aloud. Place the names of the players in the correct rows in column three, opposite their items.

Finally, after the answers have been revealed, it's time for the Bonus Surprise Points! Every player votes for one person who she thinks has the most surprising "I'm a Fan" item. This is completely up to each player, but players cannot vote for themselves. Players simply look at columns one and three for the correct matches and circle the player in column three who surprised them the most with her "I'm a Fan" item.

Now repeat the entire process, creating three-column charts for the "I'm Not a Fan" items, pulling the items from the hat, and guessing. Tally up the points for both categories to determine the overall winner.

With Only Four Players

With only four players in the game, you might decide to do both categories at once. In other words, each player places both of her items in one hat, and then everyone picks out two random pieces. Both of the items drawn may be "I'm a Fan" items or both may be "I'm Not a Fan" items. That doesn't matter. It is up to the rest of the group to determine who said it and in which category it belongs. Each player makes a numbered list from 1 to 8 (4 players × 2 items each). Players then take turns reading both of their pieces. Players must guess not only the name but also the category, and must place both pieces of information next to the appropriate item in column two. (For example, next to each item in column two, you would put "Jack, Fan" or "Taylor, Not a Fan," and so on.) This provides a much greater challenge with fewer players.

SCORING:

If your guess in column two matches with the correct answer in column three, you receive 1 point. In other words, players earn 1 point for every correct match. In addition, players receive two extra points for each "Most Surprising" vote they get!

I'm a Fan	My Guesses	Correct Answer
Pulp Fiction	Rocky	Rocky ✓
Chocolate Chip Cookies	Lisa	Rose ✗
Peanut Butter and Tomato Sandwich	Marvin	Marvin ✓ SURPRISE POINT
Cheddar Cheese/ Ranch Dressing	Rose	Lindsay ✗
Salsa Dancing	Lindsay	Brian ✗
Ping-Pong	Brian	Lisa ✗

TRIFECTA

4+
PLAYERS

//

HOW WELL DO THE OTHER PLAYERS KNOW YOU?

Note: This game can only be played if there are not complete strangers to your group participating. It is mostly for those groups of people who know each other fairly well, like friends and family members.

PREPARATION:

First, one player writes the name of every player in the group on separate pieces of paper, then folds each one, mixes them up, and places them all in a hat or face-down on a table. Next, each player must come up with an activity he thinks would typically not be associated with or attempted by a member of the group—for example, activities such as "nude sunbathing" or "eating bugs" or "hiking to the top of the tallest mountain in the world" or "walking on fire" or "crashing a wedding" or "entering a hot dog–eating contest." (Some of these activities may not be a big deal for certain members of the group, so players must be creative and come up with activities that will be out of the norm for the specific group.)

OBJECTIVE:

Players must predict the group's consensus about the tendencies and willingness of each individual to engage in certain activities.

GAME TIME:

Once everyone has thought of the activity they wish to present, Player 1 announces his activity. Then Player 1 picks two random names form the hat and reveals them. Every player then writes down the activity and lists three people next to it. The first is the person in the entire group each player thinks is "most likely" to engage in the activity. The second is the person in the entire group each player thinks is "least likely" to engage in the activity. The third is the person out of the two random people selected from the hat who would be most likely to engage in that activity (out of those two only). Players may select themselves for "most" or "least" for any given activity, if they think it's the "right" answer. Keep in mind that each player is trying to match the answers of the rest of the group, so answers should depend on what each player feels everyone in the group would say. Once everyone has written their answers, each player reveals their list. Players who match all three answers with another player achieve a trifecta match and the points are tallied accordingly (see "Scoring" below).

Player 2 then presents her activity and picks two random people from the hat, and then everyone writes down their three selections as before. The game continues until everyone has presented an interesting activity and revealed who they think is most or least likely to participate. There are endless activities you can come up with in this game.

SCORING:

Players earn 5 points for every trifecta match they achieve with another person in the group! All three names must be in the exact same order to be a match. Players do not receive any points if even one of the three is in a different order. (For example, if Player 1 had Sandy for "most likely," Phil for "least likely," and Jennifer for "more likely than Phil," (Jennifer and Phil being the two selected from the hat), and Players 5 and 6 also had those three in that same order, all three of them would earn 10 points, because each of them matched all three exactly with two other people.)

EXAMPLE:

For the activity "eating bugs," the two people pulled from the hat are Bob and Mary. Player 1's answer may be "Most: John. Least: Allison. More: Bob," and Player 2 might say "Most: John. Least: Betty. More: Bob." Both had John as "most likely" and Bob as "more likely than Mary," but because they had a different person as "least likely" in the entire group (Player 1 guessing Allison and Player 2 guessing Betty), they do not get the points!

MY DREAM HOME

3+
PLAYERS

THE DECISION OF A LIFETIME

PREPARATION:

Each player comes up with five places (specific cities, towns, or villages *only*) in the world that they have been to and like. These are places they would definitely love to live, or at least vacation in for a certain period of time. Each player also selects one location (city, town, or village) they have lived in or visited for a certain period of time but definitely *do not* want to return to or live in, even for a day. List all six of these locations on a piece of paper in random order—five desired locations and one undesired location. Players place their lists in front of them face-down.

> **Note:** Players can also list places they haven't been to but would *like* to live and *wouldn't like* to live, particularly those players who haven't done a lot of traveling.

OBJECTIVE:

To figure out the level of interest each player has in each of her selected locations.

Player 1 goes first and reads all six of her locations on her list. It is important not to give away which of the six locations is the undesirable. Every player writes down Player 1's locations on their own pieces of paper. Player 2 now selects one of the locations on Player 1's list to eliminate. Everyone, including Player 1, now crosses out that location. Player 3 selects another location to eliminate on Player 1's list. Everyone crosses out that location, as well. Now there are four locations left and Player 1 will have to rank them while everyone else will try to match Player 1's exact order. Each player will have the chance to do this with the four locations they end up with after two of the six from their lists are eliminated. However, there are specific rules for ranking the four locations.

First, the understanding is that you would have to live in *only* these four places for the rest of your life, without any chance to travel anywhere else.

- Your number one location is where you will be spending thirty-two weeks of your life every year.
- Your number two location is where you will be spending sixteen weeks of your life every year.
- Your number three location is where you will be spending three weeks of your life every year.
- Your number four location is where you will be vacationing each year for one week.

The specific time of year you spend in each place can change each year and is up to you, but you may not leave any of these four places at any time while you are there.

When Player 1 is ranking her four, every other player is trying to determine Player 1's ranking as well. Everyone writes their answers down. Once everyone is finished, pens go down and Player 1 reveals and explains her order.

Player 1 can only score if at least one person matches her order exactly! If that happens, Player 1 receives 50 points.

The guessers get 10 points for every position they get right and a bonus 10 points for getting all four. Therefore, if you get the ranking order exactly right for one player, you get the maximum 50 points. The only other options are 0, 10 or 20. For example, Player 1's list was as follows: 1. Paris 2. Florence 3. Las Vegas 4. Chicago. If Player 2 had Paris and Florence correct but Las Vegas and Chicago were switched, Player 2 would get 20 points. If Player 3 only had Chicago in the correct position and the others were wrong, Player 3 would get 10 points.

Important: After your four locations are determined, you must not give any hints as to how you will rank them!

NEXT:

Player 2 reads his list of six locations. Players 3 and 4 eliminate two of them and everyone tries to predict Player 2's ranking.

YUCK!

3+ PLAYERS

IT'S GREAT TO BE UNIQUE

PREPARATION:

Each player comes up with five things he either doesn't like at all or has never tried, seen, or tasted in his life. It can be a food, an activity, a movie, a show, a book, a concert, a person, and so on.

> **Note:** When coming up with these five things, it is important to keep in mind that they should be things you're pretty certain other people in the group have seen, tried, tasted, and so on, and *don't* dislike. The more people that aren't in the same boat as you with each of your entries, the more points you get!

Place each of the five items on separate pieces of paper and mix them with all of the others in a hat or on the table, face-down.

OBJECTIVE:

A player scores as many points as possible by getting the most people to *not* raise their hands for his five items.

Player 1 goes first and turns over the first item from the top of the pile and reads it aloud. The rule is simple: If a player either truly dislikes the item *or* has never seen, tried or tasted it, he must raise his hand! However, if he has tried it and doesn't dislike it, he must keep his hand down!

For example, let's say the item is "Shrimp." If you have tried shrimp and don't dislike it, you must keep your hand down. It doesn't mean you have to really like or love shrimp; it simply means you've tried it and you don't mind eating it at all. If the item is *Star Wars* and you've never seen it, you must raise your hand. If you have seen it and didn't like it at all, you must raise your hand as well! Again, if the item is a person or thing you don't know, a food or activity you've never tried, or a place you've never visited, you must raise your hand! For each item, the person who entered it will have his hand up. Once all hands are up, the person who entered the item reveals it was his and counts the people who have their hands down. The number of hands *not* raised for an item entered is the number of points received for that item. Don't reveal who entered it until all hands are raised. Players write down their own points on their cards.

> **Important:** It is perfectly okay if two or more people submit the same item in a round. They will simply receive the same amount of points for that item one time. Discard the item if it appears a second time.

SCORING:

The player with the most cumulative points wins the round.

NEXT:

Everyone enters five new items for round two. Players may not enter an item that has already been used! Play as many rounds as desired.

THUMBS

4–8
PLAYERS

COMBINING STRATEGY WITH DISCOVERY

PREPARATION:

None.

OBJECTIVE:

Offer up a subject which will get an agreement from all but one, and the one cannot be you! Accomplish this simple task and earn the point.

GAME TIME:

This can be a very simple game played at dinner with no writing. Take turns coming up with something that everyone agrees upon except one person. For example, if you select the movie *Forrest Gump*, once everyone knows their answer, at the count of three each player holds a thumb up, thumb down or thumb sideways. Thumbs up means *Forrest Gump* is a movie you like. Thumbs down means you don't like *Forrest Gump*. However, thumb sideways means you either haven't seen *Forrest Gump* or it didn't really make a good or bad impression on you either way. You must always tell the truth in this game. If you like it, then you must put your thumb up, and so on. You must always put your thumb sideways if you don't know the subject/item, or haven't tried or seen it. For example, if the item is shrimp and you have never even tried shrimp, you must put your thumb sideways. In addition, if you're indifferent about shrimp (don't really like it or hate it), you must put your thumb sideways as well. Movies, TV shows, or actors and actresses are always popular, but you can also use specific foods or even activities, such as playing chess, painting, or riding a bike. Anything goes! The object, however, is to get everyone to agree except for one person, and that person who doesn't agree *cannot be you*! The scoring system completely determines the strategy.

SCORING:

If there are five people in the game and you said *Forrest Gump*, you only get the one point if everyone had their thumbs one way and someone other than you had it another way. Any scenario other than that and you don't get the point. The reason the person coming up with the item can't be the only one who is different is to prevent that person from coming up with an item where he is absolutely certain he will be the only one with a thumb up, down, or sideways. That's too easy. So, if Player 1 comes up with "Riding roller coasters" and everyone but Player 2 has their thumbs up, Player 1 gets the point for coming up with something where everyone agreed except for one person.

NEXT:

Play continues with Player 2 giving her item, and so on.

ON MY ISLAND

2+
PLAYERS

//

IF YOU ONLY HAD ONE CHOICE . . . OVER AND OVER AND OVER AGAIN

PREPARATION:

None.

OBJECTIVE:

Find out the absolute favorites of the people in your group in many categories.

GAME TIME:

This is the only game in this collection of games with no winners or winning objective, no points, no strategy, and no time limit. With this game, all you need to do is to ask the following question to the group and everyone fills in the blank: "If you were placed on a deserted island for one year and you could bring one _____ with you, what would it/he/she be?

The blank could be something or someone in any number of categories. Here are some fun examples we have enjoyed through the years:

- Comedian
- Actor

- Actress
- Movie
- TV series
- Book
- World leader
- Famous person, dead or alive
- Band or Group (They can only perform their own music every day)
- Singer (Same as above)
- Athlete (They can only play the sport they are known for with you every day)
- Meal (You could only eat this one specific meal every day for a year)
- Dessert (You can only eat this one specific dessert every day for a year)
- A professional to teach you a certain skill (No need to name the professional, just the skill you would want to learn)
- Drink
- Video game
- Broadway show (The same cast would perform only their show every day)

You can make this question easier by allowing two or three choices for a category. For example, the two or three people or things you bring would rotate. You can also limit the amount of time you would get to spend with anyone or anything you bring.

The answers always tend to be interesting and you usually learn many new things about the people in your group. This game can easily be played with just two people.

WE CRACK OURSELVES UP

These games are all about getting your creative juices flowing and making people laugh—and I mean *really* laugh! For some, that may come more easily than for others. Either way, you should all have a lot of fun creating new words, phrases, stories, and illustrations that will be very hard to forget.

JIMMY PLAYED WITH BETTY'S NOSTRILS (JPWBN)

GET CREATIVE WITH ACRONYMS

PREPARATION:

Player 1 begins and comes up with any letter and announces it. Player 2 comes up with a second letter. Player 3 comes up with another, and so on until there are five letters. All players write the letters down at the top of a piece of paper in the order they were provided. Players also number a separate sheet of paper vertically, from one to the total number of players in the game.

OBJECTIVE:

Each player must come up with the most creative sentence from five randomly selected letters to earn the most votes and, thus, the most points.

GAME TIME:

Each player in the game must now come up with a creative, five-word sentence using those starting letters in the order they were given.

Important: The sentences don't need to make sense, but be sure to write clearly and legibly. Someone will need to be able to read your sentence, and you don't want people passing around your sentence for clarification!

When everyone is finished, all players crumple their sentence into a ball and place it in the middle of the table, and Player 1 mixes them up. Now each player randomly picks one up to read.

Player 1 writes the number 1 on the first sentence, announces, "Here is sentence number one," and reads it aloud without revealing who she thinks wrote the sentence. (The authors will not be revealed until the very end.) After Player 1 reads the first sentence, each player (including Player 1) writes the sentence down next to number 1 on his paper. Player 2 then writes the number 2 on the sentence he has, announces that it is sentence number two, and reads it aloud for everyone to write down next to number 2. Continue like this until all sentences have been read. Every player then looks at them all again and votes for the top two most creative, interesting, or funny sentences. (If there are more than eight players in the game, everyone should vote for the top three sentences.)

One at a time, each player reveals which two sentences she wants to vote for, and Player 1 (or the player leading the round) tallies points. After the authors reveal themselves and points are awarded, the next round begins. For the next round, Player 2 selects the first letter, Player 3 selects the next, and so on.

Note: You cannot vote for your own sentence!

The person with the sentence that receives the most votes earns 20 points, second place earns 10, and third earns 5. If there is a tie for first, each of those players gets 20 points, second place earns 10 points, and there is no third place. If there is a tie for second, each of those players gets 10 points, and there is no third place.

EXAMPLE:

Let's say the letters for this round, in order of selection from Player 1 to Player 5, are JPWBN. For these letters, one might say "Jimmy played with Betty's nostrils," or "Joanne painted Wally's blue newt," or "Joe Pesci wanted bigger napkins." Be as creative as possible.

SAMPLE:

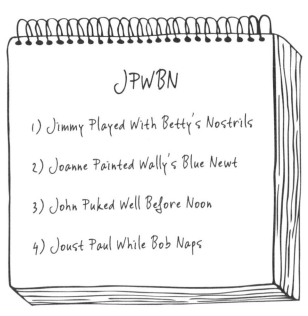

JPWBN

1) Jimmy Played With Betty's Nostrils

2) Joanne Painted Wally's Blue Newt

3) John Puked Well Before Noon

4) Joust Paul While Bob Naps

JOHN WANTED SALLY TO PLAY DEAD

> ## GETTING THE GROUP TO PUT YOUR SENTENCE BACK TOGETHER

PREPARATION:

Player 1 begins and comes up with any letter and announces it. Player 2 comes up with a second letter. Player 3 comes up with a third letter. These three letters represent the first letters of three words at the beginning of a sentence. Place them at the top of one small sheet of paper or card. The next player comes up with a fourth letter, then the next a fifth, and then finally a sixth letter from the next player. Those three letters represent the first letters of three words at the end of a sentence. Put those three letters at the top of a separate small sheet of paper or card. Each player should now have two sheets of paper with three letters at the top.

OBJECTIVE:

Each player must come up with the most creative sentence from the six randomly selected letters. The sentences will be split into two parts. Each player wants the other players in the group to find their two sections, put them together, and select their complete six-word sentence as the top choice.

Each player should have two sheets of paper with three letters at the top. Let's say the three letters for the beginning of the sentence are JWS and the three letters for the end of the sentence are TPD. As in the title of this game, one option for a sentence could be "John wanted Sally to play dead." The sentence must be in the order the letters were given! Another option could be, "Just waxed Sam's Toyota Prius, Dad!" or, "Join William Saturday to Party Down."

Players write the first three words of their sentence under the three beginning letters on their paper. In the above example, it would be JWS. They write the last three words of their sentence under the three ending letters on the other paper. In this example, it would be TPD.

Each player now hands their JWS words to one player to mix up and read in random order, and their TPD words to another player to mix up and read in random order. Two players will be the designated readers for each round. In this case, one will read all of the JWS sentence beginnings. The other will read all of the TPD sentence endings. Those players will read them slowly, so everyone can write them all down. Once each player has all of the beginning and ending options, she must decide which beginning she likes for a specific ending and make one choice. She cannot decide to use her own beginning or ending. It is certainly possible to choose the beginning of one person's sentence and the end of another person's. That will just depend on sentence construction. Either way, each player will make a final decision about a full sentence she likes the most based on putting together a beginning and end.

One at a time, players read their chosen sentences!

When one of your three-word combinations is used by another player, you receive a point. If your entire sentence
is used by a player, you earn 2 points. So, if three players
selected your entire sentence, you get 6 points. If another
player used the ending of your sentence with someone else's
beginning, that's another point for you, for a total of 7 points
for that round.

> **Important:** You don't want to give anything away if
> you figure out who wrote any of the parts of sentences.
> No names are on the pages. It's really best to not know
> who wrote them so there is no voting influence. The
> only players who may have a clue are those who are
> elected to read the options at the beginning. However,
> each of those players is only reading one part of each
> player's sentence.

NEXT:

New letters are determined randomly from the group for
round two.

FUN WITH BOB

4+
PLAYERS

SOMETHING ABOUT BOB AND A STRAWBERRY

PREPARATION:

One player is elected to write the name of each player in the game on separate pieces of paper or cards and submit them to a pile on the table. Another player is elected to write the numbers eleven to twenty on separate pieces of paper in another pile on the table. Finally, every player selects his own category, such as animals, fruits, vegetables, tools, body parts, and so on. In each category, players write three items on separate pieces of paper and put them in their own pile in front of them. For example, if your category is fruit, you can put strawberry, kiwi, and pomegranate on your three pieces of paper.

OBJECTIVE:

To come up with the most creative sentence using the person selected from the pile, the exact number of words chosen from the number pile, and the exact object from the pile of the player who determines that object in each round.

Player 1 selects a random name from the name pile. Then he selects a random number from the 11–20 number pile, and finally he announces his category and selects a random item from his own category pile. For example, let's say Player 1 selects "Jordan" from the name pile, the number "14" from the number pile, and "pomegranate" from his own pile of fruits. Every player in the game must now come up with a story in either one, two, or three sentences about Jordan and a pomegranate in exactly fourteen words. Players should be as creative as possible and include whatever other people or things they want in their story. It is all about making the best use of those items that everyone else has while keeping it to the exact amount of words, and then getting votes from the other members in the group. Players submit their finished stories to the pile. Make sure it is legible! Players should write their name on it in case the person who picks it out can't read something and asks for clarification. Every player picks one randomly from the pile to read it. If a word can't be read, then the player must ask that player for clarification and make the correction on the page. They must all be placed back in the pile and everyone picks again. This is simply to avoid voter influence. Only the author should know whose sentence it is as it is being read. Therefore, make sure stories are legible the first time! Players take turns reading the sentences they picked as everyone takes notes on the stories they like most. Once each story is read twice, players vote by going around the room and selecting the two people who read the stories they liked most. When someone selects a story the player who read it must note it on the story with a check mark. Players cannot vote for their own story!

SCORING:

Each player announces how many votes the story he read received in order to determine first, second, and third place.

The player with the most votes receives 20 points, second place receives 10 points, and third place receives 5 points. In a tie for first place, those players all receive 20 points, second place earns 10 points, and there is no third place. In a tie for second place, those players all receive 10 points and then there is no third place. Authors of the winning stories are revealed.

RUMORS

4+ PLAYERS

HEARD IT FROM A FRIEND WHO HEARD IT FROM A FRIEND

PREPARATION:

Each player makes up crazy rumors about anyone or anything and puts each one on a separate paper or index card, placing it face-down on the table or in a hat. Players shouldn't let anyone see their rumors, and they should be one or two sentences maximum. Something like, "Forty aliens named Burt were arrested in Pittsburgh," or, "They just found two tons of Muenster cheese on the moon." Players can enter up to three different rumors per round and must enter at least one, writing legibly and including their name at the top of each rumor.

OBJECTIVE:

To create rumors which will be voted on by the rest of the group as one of the top two.

GAME TIME:

Player 1 is elected to read all of the rumors, numbering them as she reads them. First, she must count them while they are face-down. If there are fewer than ten different rumors, then she will leave them in one pile. With ten or more, she must

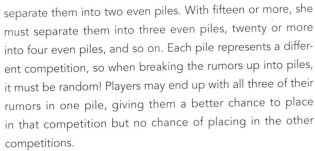

separate them into two even piles. With fifteen or more, she must separate them into three even piles, twenty or more into four even piles, and so on. Each pile represents a different competition, so when breaking the rumors up into piles, it must be random! Players may end up with all three of their rumors in one pile, giving them a better chance to place in that competition but no chance of placing in the other competitions.

For each pile, Player 1 reads all of the rumors, numbering them while she is reading them so everyone can write them down. It's a good idea for Player 1 to read all the rumors to herself first, so she can ask for clarification from the writers if needed. Player 1 will read them all twice, without revealing the authors. Each player, including Player 1, writes down the numbers of the two she likes the best. Players cannot choose their own! Player 1 asks everyone for their numbers out loud, records them, and adds her own votes, then comes up with the final tally for first and second place. If there is another pile, she then reads all of those rumors and repeats the process. She repeats it for each pile until there are winners of each. Authors are not revealed until all competitions are completed.

SCORING:

Each player starts each round of this game with 8 points. For each additional rumor you enter over one, it will cost you 4 points. So, if you enter the maximum three rumors into the competition, your point total is 0 before Player 1 begins reading the rumors in the competition. If you only submit a second rumor in a round, you start with 4 points.

When Player 1 tallies the votes for each group of rumors, first place wins 20 points and second place wins 10 points. If there is a tie for first place, each of those players gets 20 points and there will be no second place. If there is a tie for second place, each of those players gets 10 points.

NEXT:

For round two, everyone automatically adds 8 points to their score and new rumors are entered into the hat or placed on the table. Remember, players must subtract 4 points from their score for each additional rumor entered over one, and they must enter at least one rumor per round (but no more than three). Play as many rounds as desired and crown an overall winner for most points.

THAT'S DELICIOUS

WE CRACK OURSELVES UP

CREATE THE MOST CREATIVE DISHES WITH LIMITED INGREDIENTS

PREPARATION:

None.

OBJECTIVE:

To come up with the most creative meal with the letters provided for the best chance of approval from your group.

GAME TIME:

Player 1 goes first and says a random letter. (In this game, players may want to avoid the letter "X.") Player 2 says another letter, Player 3 yet another, and Player 4 finishes with a fourth letter. Those four letters must be written down by all players in the exact order they were provided, and they will be used by everyone in the game to describe a creative dish. Each letter is the first letter of a word in the dish. For example, with the letters CMAJ in the order they were provided by Players 1–4, possibilities could be "Chocolate Meatballs and Jam" or "Chopped Mango Au Jus" or "Chuck's Mustache Apple Juice." Anything goes! Players may submit one or two entries. Players write each dish legibly on a separate card without including their name. Once each player comes up with a dish or two, all submissions are placed in a pile in the middle of the table and mixed up thoroughly while face-down.

The Battle Round:

Player 1 picks out the first two dishes from the pile and reads them. He gives each one a number and everyone votes on his favorite at the count of three by holding up one or two fingers. Votes are based on creativity or most interesting dish. Players who created one of the dishes being voted on may not vote. (It's best not to reveal which of the two you wrote. Simply don't hold up any fingers if you are in the contest.) The dish with the most votes stays in the competition and is placed in a new pile. The dish that loses the vote is discarded. If there is a tie, both dishes move to the next round and are placed in the new pile. Every player should write down each dish that makes it past the battle round on a separate piece of paper. They should all be numbered in an order confirmed by Player 1.

Player 2 then picks out the next two dishes from the pile, reads them out loud, and repeats the process with the group. Player 3 reads the next two submissions, and so on until there are none left. If there is an odd number of submissions, the final dish will automatically advance to the next round after it is read to the group. Every player should now have written down all of the dishes that have made it to the final round.

Note: With more than eight players, limit the number of submissions to just one per player.

The Final Round:

The second and final round begins with Player 1 reading all of the submissions in the order in which they had advanced to the next round after winning the first-round battle. This is simply to confirm that everyone has their lists correct, with each dish assigned a number. Each player now selects his favorite of the final group. Again, his vote should be based on creativity or what he simply feels is the most interesting dish. Players may not vote for any of their own! Going around the room, each player announces the number he has selected and Player 1 keeps a tally.

> **Note:** With fewer than eight initial submissions, there is no reason to play a first battle round. Simply list them all once they are read and each player votes for his favorite.

SCORING:

The top three vote-earners earn 30, 20, and 10 points for first, second, and third place, respectively. If there is a tie for first, each of those players gets 30 points, second place earns 20 points, and there is no third place. If there is a tie for second, each of those players gets 20 points and there will be no third place.

NEXT:

A new group of four letters is offered up in order from Players 2–5.

WE FINISH EACH OTHER'S SENTENCES

//

HELP OUT THE PLAYERS IN YOUR GROUP BY COMPLETING THEIR ORIGINAL THOUGHTS

PREPARATION:

None.

OBJECTIVE:

To come up with the most creative end to a sentence from what is provided in each round. However, players are *only* trying to get approval from the subject of the sentence himself.

GAME TIME:

Player 1 comes up with the beginning of a sentence using Player 2 as the subject. The beginning of the sentence can only be a maximum of six words and must include the name of Player 2. For example, if Player 2's name is Jeff, Player 1 might say something like, "Jeff went to the store to . . ." or "Jeff was mad at Jack because . . ." or "Jeff was shocked that . . ." Player 1 announces her sentence beginning to the group. All of the players in the game, including Player 1 but not Player 2, must now get creative and finish the sentence! Every player places her finished sentence in a pile without writing her name and the pile gets mixed up. Player 1 picks them all up and reads them in random order. Nobody should reveal the sentence they wrote to avoid bias in the voting. Player 2, the subject of these sentences, writes down notes about each sentence and must determine a first and second place according to his two favorites. He announces them to the group.

SCORING:

First place gets 20 points, second place gets 10 points. Then the authors of first and second place are revealed, along with the authors of any of the others if those authors wish to do so.

NEXT:

Player 2 now offers up the beginning of a sentence with Player 3 as the subject, and play continues with round two. With six players as an example, the last round will be Player 6 providing the beginning of a sentence with Player 1 as the subject.

TELL ME A STORY

> ## WHICH OF THESE PEOPLE, PLACES, OR THINGS WILL HELP YOU CREATE A SHORT STORY FOR THE AGES?

PREPARATION:

With fewer than ten players, each player must write down two different people, places, or things and submit them to the hat or pile on the table. The people, places, or things can be anything—they can even be completely made-up. However, each player wants the other players to select his items for their story. Therefore, be creative! Players should submit items they feel will be the most tempting for players to include. Each person, place or thing should be on a separate paper or card, and they are mixed all together in one pile. With ten or more players, each player should submit only one person, place, or thing to the pile. Players do not include their names on the papers.

OBJECTIVE:

To come up with the most creative short story from the three items chosen in each round, which leads to strong approval from the group, and also to submit items that the other players choose for their stories.

With fewer than ten players, each player picks two random pieces of paper or cards from the pile. With ten or more, each player picks one. Each player looks at the items on the card(s), writes down the items on a separate piece of paper, and passes the items to the left. Players are simply taking notes in order to decide which *three* items they will use for their story. Once all items are seen by everyone, those items are placed back in a pile on the table or discarded. Each player must now quickly decide which three items from the other players he wants to use in his story. Players may not use any of their own submissions! Once players have decided, the timekeeper puts five minutes on the clock. Each player will now *very legibly* write a story, which must be at least twenty words and no more than fifty words. Keep to the minimum and do not exceed the maximum! This simply keeps the game fair. Each player must also use *only three* of the items presented by the group. Players may not use more than three, and they must use all three. If not, the story will be disqualified. Players submit their story to a new pile on the table, putting their name at the top just in case someone has trouble reading it.

After mixing up the stories, each player picks one out of the pile at random. Players go around the room reading the stories they have as everyone takes notes on stories they like most. In addition, if a player hears one of his items being used in a story, he must note it! He receives a point every time one of his items is used in a story. Players should read each story twice. Just go around the room two times. Once each story is read twice, players vote by going around the room and selecting the two people who read the stories they liked most. (Only vote for one person with fewer than five players.) When someone selects a story as a favorite, the player who read it must note it on the story with a check mark. Players cannot vote for the story they wrote, but they can certainly vote for the story they read if it isn't their own!

Each player announces the votes received for the story he read in order to determine first, second, and third place. First place receives 10 points, second place receives 5 points, and third place receives 3 points. In the event of a tie for first, those players each receive 10 points, second place receives 5 points, and there is no third place. A tie for second and those players each receive 5 points—in that case, there will also be no third place. Authors of the winning stories are revealed and receive their points. Then come the bonus points. In addition, each player (whether or not he placed for his own story) receives a point for every item he submitted that was used in another story. Therefore, you may still receive a lot of points for the round if people used your items, even if you didn't have one of the winning stories. If one of your items was used in five different stories, you receive 5 points for that item alone!

WE CRACK OURSELVES UP

DRAW THIS!

4+
PLAYERS

///

THAT WORK OF ART NEEDS NO EXPLANATION

PREPARATION:

Every player thinks of two famous people and writes each of them on a separate piece of paper, placing them in a pile with all the others. These people should be well-known to everyone in the group. Next, each player thinks of two activities—things such as riding a bike, walking a dog, playing chess, or driving a race car.

> **Important:** The activities shouldn't be too complicated. You may end up having to draw one of them, and you don't want it to be too much of a challenge!

Each player writes the two activities on separate pieces of paper and places them in a big activities pile, separate from the famous people pile on the table. Someone is in charge of mixing both piles up separately and leaving them facedown. On another piece of paper, each player should make a list of the names of all the players in the game, with enough room to the right of each name to fill in guesses. Finally, each player should have another blank piece of paper to make a drawing.

To create a work of art which can be summed up very easily, a drawing in which nobody will struggle to figure out who it is and what the person is doing.

Each player picks two random items from the famous people pile and two random items from the activities pile, without revealing their picks to anyone. Once players have their four items, they will now have a choice of which famous person of the two they will draw and which of the two activities that person will be doing. They must choose from the two selections. No asking for another option! They have five minutes to make the drawing. There can be no words on the drawing, with only one exception: a speech bubble coming from the famous person's mouth. There can only be two words in the speech bubble, and neither of those words can be any part of the name of the person or the activity. That is the only additional hint everyone else gets in figuring out the drawing. Players write their name at the top of their drawing. When the five minutes are up, the guessing begins! At the count of three, each player passes his drawing to the person to her right. Players will now take thirty seconds to look at the drawing and write down who they think the famous person and activity are, next to the player's name who drew the picture on the list of players in the game. At thirty seconds, every player passes the drawing to the right again, and they repeat the process of writing down a guess as to who it is and what the person is doing. Once players receive their original drawing back, they will have noted a guess for every player's drawing. Then the scoring begins.

WE CRACK OURSELVES UP

Pass your paper with the guesses to the person next to you. That person will score your guesses. Player 1 begins by announcing what her person and activity are on her drawing. Players raise their hands if the card in front of them has the correct guess. Each player who guessed correctly gets 1 point. In addition, Player 1 gets a point for every player who guessed her exact person and activity. No partial credit! You must have both correct! Player 2 then reveals his person and activity, records how many people got his right, and gives himself those points. So, you get a point for each drawing you guess right, and you get a point for each player who guesses your person and activity. Therefore, if you get three right and four people guess your drawing correctly, you have a total of 7 points for that round.

> **Important Rule:** When submitting famous people to the pile, you can use animated characters if you like. However, you can't submit fictional characters played by actors, such as Princess Leia or Han Solo. You would have to submit Carrie Fisher or Harrison Ford. The artist could certainly draw Princess Leia or Han Solo to get people to figure out the actors.

ALTER EGO

HAVING FUN ON OPPOSITE DAY

PREPARATION:

The preparation for this game will take about five to ten minutes. The responsibility of each player is to create a fun and creative image of a very different version of a day in the life of two players in the game. So, Player 1 will be creating a day for the player to his left and another one for the player to his right. Player 2 will do the same for the two players sitting next to her, and so on.

For each subject, players must make a list of five items on separate pieces of paper. They must be legible because the subjects will have to read them out loud. The first item on the list is what the subject will want everyone to call him on that day. The second item is what the subject will decide to wear that day. The third item is the subject's mode of transportation to work that day. The fourth item is the subject's occupation, and the last item is the subject's evening activity.

All five of these things should either create an image of a day which would be the complete opposite of the typical life of that person, or simply a fun, strange, or interesting version of that person.

Once every player has created a profile for the person to his left and right, he hands that profile to the subject. So,

Player 1 will hand the profile he created for the person to his left to him, and the profile he created for the person to his right to her. Everyone does the same.

Now every player should have two sheets of paper outlining an "Alter Ego" which has been created for him. He should read each one to himself first and ask questions quietly to the writers if he has trouble understanding any item he is reading.

OBJECTIVE:

For each subject, come up with the most creative name, attire, mode of transportation to work, daytime occupation, and evening activity to earn the most points.

GAME TIME:

Player 1 goes first and begins by reading two options for what he wants everyone to call him on his new day. He will say something like this: "Today I want everyone to either call me 'Skinny Pete' or 'Hot tub Harry.'" These are the two choices he was given by the people to his left and right. Now everyone writes those down. He then continues with his two wardrobe choices by saying what he sees on each paper: "I will either be wearing 'A toga' or 'A pair of pink stockings, a cowboy hat, and a tool belt.'" Everyone writes those down as well. Play continues until all five category options are provided. Everyone, except Player 1 and the two authors of his profile, now has sixty seconds to choose which options in each category they feel would make the best "Alter Ego" for Player 1. Throughout the process of providing the choices for each of the five categories, Player 1 should not reveal the author of either option to avoid bias in voting. He should always be mixing his choices up and providing them in random order so nobody knows who gave him each item. Once every judge determines which items she is choosing for Player 1, players take turns revealing their selections. Let's say Player 4 goes first. He says, "My day for Player 1 begins with him asking everyone to call him Skinny Pete. Then he will put on a toga, leave for work driving a forklift, and arrive at his job of teaching old people in a nursing home how to play dodgeball. Then he will return home and give his pet monkey a foot massage." Player 5 will then read the selections he made for Player 1, and so on, until all players have gone.

SCORING:

Each of the two players who gave an "Alter Ego" day to Player 1 receives one point every time one of her items was selected by any player. For example, with six total players in the game, there are always three people voting and a total of 15 points up for grabs for the authors of Player 1's "Alter Ego" day. (5 categories × 3 players.) No points for Player 1; he is merely the subject. No points for the judges, either. The only players competing for points on Player 1's round are the two authors of his "Alter Ego" day.

NEXT:

Player 2 is the next subject and reads her "Alter Ego" day options given to her by the players to her left and right. Play continues until every player takes her turn.

LET YOUR IMAGINATION GO WILD

PREPARATION:

Each player creates a fun short story in a sentence or two about one or more people in the group. The very short story must be thirty-five words or fewer and must include at least five verbs. Players write their story out on a piece of paper or index card without letting anyone see and underline the five verbs. They turn their card over.

OBJECTIVE:

To receive the most cumulative points by coming up with the most fun and creative story in each round using the verbs provided.

GAME TIME:

Player 1 turns over her card first and reads *only* the five verbs she underlined in her story to the rest of the group. The verbs must be provided in the same tense they are used in Player 1's sentence. Every other player must write those verbs down in the order they were provided. A five-minute timer is set. Every other player must now fill in the blanks with a story of thirty-five words or fewer using the verbs Player 1 announced and in the order in which they were provided. The verbs must be used in the same tense, as well. For example, let's say Player 1 gave the following verbs: "went, buy, skipped, singing, telling." Every other player must now fill in the blanks with a story using those *same exact* words. Players may not exchange the word "buy" for the past tense "bought," or "skipped" for "skipping," or "singing" for "sing." So, your sentence could be something like, "Jamie **went** crazy when Lucy asked her to **buy** more deodorant. She **skipped** class, then told Lucy to stop **singing** because it was awful and she was **telling** mom on her." Or, "Bob and Russell **went** to the drug store to **buy** anti-aging cream for Phil. They **skipped** there, **singing** Beatles songs and **telling** secrets about their grandmothers." Anything goes, as long as the words provided are in the same order and the story is thirty-five words or fewer. Write legibly!

Player 2 collects all of the stories, including the original one written by Player 1. Player 2 mixes them all up and reads them randomly out loud to the group. Player 2 numbers them so there is a specific order for voting purposes. Each player writes down a few words from each story for memory and then votes on the one he likes the best by circling the number. Players cannot vote for their own! Player 2 can repeat the stories a second time if requested. Next, each player gives the number he voted for to Player 2 to write down and tally the votes.

SCORING:

The player who writes the original story in each round receives 1 point per vote received. The other players receive 2 points per vote received. For example, if Player 1 provided the verbs in her original story (as in the case above) and receives a total of 3 votes, she receives 3 points. However, if Player 2 receives

2 votes for the story he told with Player 1's verbs, Player 2 receives 4 points. Since it is a more difficult task to come up with a creative story using someone else's words, you get more credit for coming up with a story that was recognized as even more fun or interesting than the original.

NEXT:

Player 2 shares the five underlined verbs in his story with the other players and every other player has five minutes to come up with a story using those verbs in the order they were provided. Player 3 collects them all, reads them, and tallies the votes.

WE CRACK OURSELVES UP

WORDICULOUS

4+ PLAYERS

CREATE A WINNING DEFINITION

PREPARATION:

Each player makes up a fun word that someone else will have to define and submits it to a pile face-down in the middle of the table with all the others. Someone mixes them all up.

OBJECTIVE:

Create a definition that will receive the most votes.

GAME TIME:

Each player selects a random word from the pile and now has to write a definition under the word on the front of the card. It is OK if a player happens to select his own word, but the selection should be random. Players have no more than two minutes to come up with the definition, then place the card back in the middle of the table, face-down and mixed with all the others. One player is then assigned to write a number on the back of each card, from one to however many people are in the game. That player then distributes the cards to all the players in order. Each player then reads the word and definition he received while the other players can make notes for voting. Once the last player reads his word and definition, the voting begins. Each player gives the scorekeeper the number of the word and definition pair he liked the best. Players must vote for their favorite *pair*, voting on which word and definition combination they like best. Players cannot vote for their own word (even if they like the new definition best), or their own definition.

SCORING:

You score a point every time someone selects your word or definition. So, if three people select your word and someone else's definition, you score three points, and if two people select your definition for someone else's word, you score another 2 points. If you happen to have written a definition for your own word, you can score 2 points for every person who selects that card. On the other hand, writing a definition for your own word could put you at risk of not scoring any points at all if your word and definition are not popular.

SPILL THE BEANS

MAKING UP SLANG FOR THE NEXT GENERATION

PREPARATION:

Write each letter of the alphabet on separate cards, then place all of the consonants in one pile and the vowels in another pile.

OBJECTIVE:

To come up with the most creative new slang from the combination of letters provided in each round.

GAME TIME:

Someone is elected to pick out two random consonants and one random vowel from the two piles. For example, you may end up with RAP, STA, TEL, MOF, DIB, VUN, and so on. Now everyone has five minutes to make up one to three new slang terms with the combination of letters selected (in any order), as well as a definition of each new slang term. For example, with RAP you can start your slang term with PRA, PAR, ARP, APR, RAP, or RPA. They simply have to be the first three letters of some made-up term you submit, with your made-up definition underneath. Just make sure it is something new and not a term that already exists, such as "Chill Out," "Couch Potato," "Hang Out," "Bail," "Going Dutch," "Shoot the Breeze," "Crash," and so on.

With fewer than six players, each player can submit up to three different made-up slang terms and definitions. With six or more players, each player can submit up to two different terms. Players don't have to submit more than one if they don't want to. Make sure each term and definition is legible! Otherwise, it may not be included. Place them all in a pile face-down without a name on them, and mix them all up with all of the others.

Player 1 is then selected to read them all. However, Player 1 must separate the pile into groups of three, four, or five submissions each. Make the fewest groups possible. For example, if there are a total of five entries, one group of five is it. If there are six entries, two groups of three. For seven entries do groups of four and three. For twelve entries, three groups of four works perfectly. Groups of four and five are best for better competition, but Player 1 can separate them however she likes. Player 1 does not look at the submissions when she is separating them into groups.

Player 1 will then read the submissions from the first group out loud, numbering them as she reads them, and players will write down the terms and definitions if necessary to remember them all for the vote. Player 1 will then quickly read them all again, one more time. Once they are all read twice, at the count of three, each player (including Player 1) will vote for her favorite in the group by holding up fingers. Player 1 keeps a tally and will announce the winner with the most votes. Players cannot vote for their own!

In addition, nobody should reveal which ones are his when Player 1 is reading them, just to avoid any voting influence. Player 1 shouldn't hint at that either, if she has a clear idea.

Player 1 then reads all of the submissions for the second group and the same voting process continues, for that group and every group after that depending upon how many groups of submissions there are in each round.

SCORING:

The player who gets the most votes in each group earns 5 points. If there is a tie, each player gets 5 points. Obviously, the more submissions, the better chance you have to score in each round. There's even the possibility that all of your submissions win if you end up with one in each group. Since the selection of submissions for each group is random, you may also get stuck with all of your submissions in one group.

NEXT:

A new group of three starting letters and new made-up slang terms and definitions are created for round two. Player 2 will divide them into groups and read them.

WE CRACK OURSELVES UP

These games are all about bringing out your inner actor. A chance to take the stage for even a few seconds and put on the performance of a lifetime which will lead to the rest of the group wondering if you missed your calling . . . or perhaps not! Either way, many will find these games to be a fun way to express yourself in a manner you rarely do, and to explore how well you can make-believe.

WHAT A PERFORMANCE

**INDEX CARDS
RECOMMENDED**

LIGHTS, CAMERA, ACTION!

PREPARATION:

Each player comes up with a number of ten-second acts he wants other players in the game to perform. That number of acts is equivalent to the number of total players in the game, minus three. So, if there are seven total players in the game, each player comes up with four ten-second acts and writes each of them on separate index cards. For example, you can write on one card, "act like you just won the championship game." On another card, "act like you just lost a pet." On another card, "flirt with another player in the game from across the room." You can tell another player to complain about someone in the game who always steals all of his food. Anything goes!

Now, if there are seven players in the game and four acts written on cards, then there are two players left without an act. (The player coming up with the acts doesn't count.) Those two players will eventually get blank cards and they will have to come up with their own performances. So, make sure there are two blank index cards ready to mix in with the others. There will always be two players coming up with their own acts. For example, with only five total players, each player will come up with two acts for people to perform, and the other two people performing will make the performances up themselves.

OBJECTIVE:

When coming up with the acts, players try to ask people to do things nobody would think they would ask. When faced with a blank card and inventing an act, players try to make it seem as if they were asked to perform this act and did not choose it.

GAME TIME:

With seven total players, Player 1 mixes his four acts with two blank index cards, then passes his cards out one at a time without letting anyone see what he is giving to each player. Player 1 must randomly pass out cards without knowing which card he is giving to each player. Once every player has a card and is looking at their instructions, Player 1 gives them all sixty seconds to think about their performances. This will specifically give time to the two players who drew blank cards to think about what they want to do. Once the sixty seconds are up, the players take turns performing the ten-second acts that are on their cards. If the card has instructions, players must do exactly what they are told. If the card is blank, anything goes. Players must not let anyone see their card! After everyone performs, all of the players except Player 1 now try to guess who had the blank cards. Each player writes on a piece of paper the names of the two people they think wrote their acts and were not directed by Player 1. Obviously, the two players who had blanks have an advantage by knowing that they have one of the blanks. They just have to figure out who the other player was.

Once everyone reveals their guesses as to which two players had the blanks, points are awarded. Every player who guessed both correctly earns 25 points. No partial credit! Points are only awarded to players who guess both blanks correctly. Player 1 earns 5 points for every player who is fooled and doesn't guess the two blanks correctly.

Tip: When performing, you want to do your best to fool people into believing *you* have the blank if you don't, and if you have one of the blanks, you want people to believe you were *told* to act the way you are acting. You want to be the only one who gets both right for the 25 points.

NEXT:

Player 2 presents her cards (with the two blanks mixed in) to the rest of the players in the game for round two.

YES, NO, MAYBE

HOW WELL CAN YOU SELL YOUR THREE DIFFERENT OPINIONS?

PREPARATION:

Each player submits three to five different activities or subjects they really like to a big pile on the table or in the hat. Each activity or subject must be on a separate piece of paper. An activity could be anything from a sport, to sewing, to pottery, to drinking coffee, and so on. A subject can be anything from a movie or TV show, to a book, to rainy days, or the smell of gasoline. Players must be honest and submit things they really enjoy. However, all of these activities or subjects should be things on which at least one other person in the group may have a completely different opinion. For instance, you shouldn't put things like "Breathing" or "Being alive." Things like that will not work in this game. Mix all of the activities and subjects submitted by everyone together.

OBJECTIVE:

Be as convincing as possible when arguing all three opinions on a selected subject or activity.

GAME TIME:

Player 1 goes first and selects two random items from the pile. If she picks an item she submitted, she must toss it and pick again. Next, she decides which of the two items she wants to play and tosses the other back into the pile.

Player 1 then writes on a small piece of paper the number 1, 2, or 3, and places it face-down in front of her without letting anyone see what she wrote. 1 means she likes it, 2 means she doesn't like it, and 3 means she is completely indifferent. If Player 1 has never tried the activity or subject, she must write number 3 for indifference.

Player 1 takes fifteen seconds to prepare, then begins. Player 1 must be very convincing for thirty seconds about how much she really likes the activity or subject she chose from the pile. After that, she must completely switch gears and talk for thirty seconds about how much she really doesn't like that same activity or subject. Finally, she must then take thirty seconds to talk about how indifferent she is about that same activity or subject. For example, if Player 1 selects Fishing, she has to argue how much she likes fishing, how much she doesn't like fishing, and how much she really doesn't care either way.

Once she is done, all players must now decide which one was the truth. At the count of three, each player guesses by putting up 1, 2, or 3 fingers, or holding up a card with one of those numbers.

Once everyone reveals their guesses, Player 1 turns over the correct answer. Players get 10 points if they were correct in their guess. Player 1 gets 40 points if there were three different answers in the group. That means that at least one person had each of the three different possibilities and Player 1 succeeded in making a convincing argument for all three. Player 1 gets 20 points if there were only two different answers among the group. Finally, she loses 10 points if everyone in the group had the same answer.

Important: Nobody in the group can speak or influence others during Player 1's ninety seconds of play, or after her time and before the final vote.

MIME

4+
PLAYERS

QUICK ON YOUR FEET
IN TOTAL SILENCE

PREPARATION:

Each player prepares four words for the player to his right which he thinks that player will easily be able to mime in a short period of time. Words such as "Hammer," "Nail," "Shoe," "Sneaker," "Computer," "Telephone," "Run," "Walk," "Smoke," "Vacuum," "Table," "Chair," "Sleep," "Blink," and so on. No body parts allowed, and the player who mimes cannot point to any object in the room or mouth the word. Players may not collaborate with the player to whom they are going to provide these words. The words will be kept a secret until the timer begins. Write each word on a separate card or piece of paper and keep them face-down in an individual pile.

OBJECTIVE:

Players come up with words that will be easy to mime and easily understood in a very short period of time for maximum points on their partner's turn, and mime the words they are given as efficiently as possible.

Players 1 and 2 go first, with Player 1 providing the four words for Player 2 to mime. Again, Player 2 may not mouth any word or point to any object in the room. Player 1 puts sixty seconds on the clock and starts the clock the second after Player 2 picks up his first of four cards in the pile placed in front of him by Player 1. He looks at his first card without showing it to anyone and then places it back on the table face-down. Player 2 then immediately indicates to the group that it is his first word by holding up one finger, and then he must do his best to mime that word until he feels everyone understands what it is. Player 2 then looks at his second card, puts it back face-down on top of the first card, and holds up two fingers indicating that this is his second word. He then mimes word number two. Again, he waits until he feels everyone has it (or at least most people) before moving on to word number three, and then word number four. While this is taking place, there should be no talking by anyone else in the game! Once Player 2 feels he is satisfied with the final mime, he says "Stop!" Player 1 then stops the timer immediately. While Player 2 is miming all of the words, the other players in the game are writing down what they believe to be each of the four words. Each player passes his guesses to the player to his right, who will score his card. Player 2 reveals the right answers. Players must answer all four correctly to receive credit!

Note: Players must exactly match the mimed word for a correct answer. If the prompt was "roller skating" and you guess "ice skating," it doesn't count. Therefore, when writing and performing mimes, you want the actions to be extremely clear. Remember, "close" only counts in horseshoes and hand grenades!

Players 1 and 2 both receive the same amount of points for miming success. That is why you want to give your partner the easiest words possible to mime. The more people who successfully figure out all four words, the more points Players 1 and 2 get. Finally, the faster the mime of all four words takes, the more points the two players obtain as well.

Here's how the scoring goes: Multiply the number of players who got all four words right by the time left on the clock from the sixty-second start, and that is the number of points Players 1 and 2 receive. For example, if Player 2 stopped the clock at fifteen seconds left and there were two players who guessed all four words correctly, the total points for Players 1 and 2 would be 30 (15 seconds × 2 players). Every player who guesses all four correctly receives 50 points! Again, a player guessing *must* get all four right to qualify for points and to give credit to Players 1 and 2. No points if you miss just one!

NEXT:

Player 2 places his four words face-down in front of Player 3, and those two players try to obtain points.

With an Odd Number of Players:

For example, if there are five players, Player 5 gives words to Player 1 and that will be the final round of the game, since each player will have provided words and mimed once, unless you decide to play more rounds.

Important: Once a word is used, it cannot be used again. Therefore, after each round, players must make sure to exchange any words they came up with which have already been mimed, with new words.

WHO IS PATTY WIGGLESWORTH?

> PRETENDING TO KNOW PEOPLE
> YOU DON'T AND GETTING A
> KICK OUT OF YOUR OPPONENT
> TRYING TO DO THE SAME

PREPARATION:

Players come up with the names of three people from their past, or people they know today, but who are completely unknown to the rest of the group. It can be anyone from a co-worker, to someone you met on a trip, to a former classmate, to a relative, or even simply a friend of a friend. Nobody else in the group should know this person or have even heard them talk about this person. Write each of the three complete names (first and last) on a separate index card written *legibly*, and place them in an individual pile.

OBJECTIVE:

Players convince everyone in the game that the people they select randomly from the pile are all people they submitted, and not anyone their opponent submitted.

Players 1 and 2 begin by combining each of the three people they know into a pile of six cards and mixing them up. At no time should either player see the names of the other player. They are to be kept face-down while they are being mixed. In addition, at no time should any of the other players in the game be able to see the names from Players 1 and 2. Those other players should also have their own names in front of them, face-down, until it is their turn to play.

Once the six cards from Players 1 and 2 are mixed up, the pile should be placed face-down in front of both of them. Play now begins.

Flip a coin to see who goes first. Let's say Player 1 goes first. Player 1 must pick up the first card from the pile. She waits twenty seconds before she may start speaking. This is to give her time to come up with a fake story about how she knows this person, in case it is a person submitted by Player 2. The twenty-second planning period is mandatory! No exceptions, even if it is your person. Player 1 first announces the name on the card to everyone and then has no more than sixty seconds to explain how she knows the person on the card. She must be as convincing as possible, whether she is telling the truth or not. Player 1 wants everyone to think she knows this person. Player 2 cannot talk during this time. Once Player 1 is done, Player 2 takes the card and must do the same. Player 2 has the same objective. He must try to convince everyone in the max sixty seconds that this person is someone that *he* knows, not Player 1, and that Player 1 is not telling the truth, regardless of what the truth really is.

Once the sixty seconds are up for Player 2, the other players can take notes on who they feel is telling the truth. Next, Player 2 picks up the next card from the top of the pile, waits twenty seconds, announces the new name, and then repeats the process by trying to convince everyone guessing that he is the one who submitted this person, and how he knows this person. Player 1 then takes her turn. Finally, Player 1 goes first on the third and final name. That's right—only three names are selected from the pile to play! This way, all three could have been submitted by Player 1, all three by Player 2, or it will be a two-to-one scenario.

Once the sixty seconds are up for Player 2 on the third person, each guessing player gets to ask either Player 1 or Player 2 a question about any of the names provided! Anything goes. The players will then have to answer the questions or risk being found out. However, each guessing player may only ask one question, to *either* Player 1 or Player 2, but not both. Once the inquisition is over, the players write down their final guesses as to which name belongs to which player and they reveal their guesses one at a time, with reasoning if they want to give it, and without a reaction from Players 1 and 2. Players cannot change their original guesses based on the reasoning provided by the players who made statements before them! The truth is then revealed by Players 1 and 2 and points are awarded. Players 1 and 2 must not react until the very end, when they actually give the correct answers.

> **Important:** During the entire process, Players 1 and 2 cannot show the cards to anyone!

SCORING:

Guessing players get 10 points for each correct guess, for a total possible 30 points. Players 1 and 2 each get 5 points for every player who guessed they were the player who knew one of the three people played, regardless of whether or not it was correct. If Player 3 guesses two of the names were submitted by Player 1 and one name from Player 2, then Player 1 gets 10 points and Player 2 gets 5 from Player 3's guesses, regardless of whether or not Player 3 was correct on any of

them. So, if Player 5 guesses Player 1 for all three but it was Player 2 who actually knew all three, Player 1 gets 15 points from Player 5, who actually ends up getting no points at all in that round, nor does Player 2 get any points from Player 5's guesses. Therefore, it is all about getting players to pick *you* for all three names for the maximum score!

Players 3 and 4 go. If there is an odd number of players, everyone can play twice. In that scenario, each player will have to come up with the names of six people they know that nobody in the group knows. So, for an example with five players, Player 2 would play with Player 3 after he plays with Player 1, and Player 5 would play with Player 1 after she plays with Player 4.

LIAR, LIAR PANTS ON FIRE

TEST YOUR ACTING SKILLS UNDER EXTREME PRESSURE!

PREPARATION:

For each round of this game, players must come up with something interesting that has happened in their lives that most people in the group don't know about; the ideal scenario in this game is for nobody to know about it.

> **Note:** For some groups, including family members, this may be a difficult task. Still, you should be able to think of something you did—some big or small event you witnessed, or perhaps someone you met (maybe even a celebrity)—that you never told anyone in your group about.

Each player writes this experience or event down in *as few words as possible* on a piece of paper with their name written underneath. For example, short phrases like "Met Bill Murray" or "Witnessed a car crash" or "Saw someone vomit on the subway" or "Got a rash from eating strawberries" or "Saw a streaker at a baseball game" work well.

Once every player has an event written down with their name, all players crumple their papers into a ball and place them in a hat with everyone else's papers. Now each player makes a numbered list (from one to the total number of players in the game) on a separate piece of paper, leaving enough room next to each number to write down the event.

OBJECTIVE:

Players try to fool other players into believing that a completely fabricated story actually happened—or that a true story is just a well-conceived lie.

GAME TIME:

One at a time, players pick out a crumpled piece of paper, and everyone opens their paper without letting anyone see what they have. Player 1 goes first and announces the event he picked, but he does not reveal the player who wrote it. Everyone writes the event down next to the number 1 on his piece of paper.

Every player, beginning with Player 2, must try to make everyone else believe that the event Player 1 announced was theirs! Every player tries to come up with a convincing story to persuade the group, then yields the floor to the next player, and so on until it gets back to Player 1, who will also take a turn convincing everyone that he was the one who actually had the experience he read aloud. Of course, one person in the group will actually be telling the truth, and that player *must* tell the truth, but he really wants everyone to believe he is making it up like everyone else in the game.

Players can decide how detailed their story will be, but every story must include three basic elements:

1. Where it happened
2. When it happened
3. Who you were with when it happened

Once every player has told their story about the event, all players write down who they think really submitted that event next to the event on their numbered page. (Players can certainly change their mind at the end of the game, but for now, they are making a note about who they think told the truth about that specific event.)

Note: The true storyteller writes his own name next to the story, and the person who picked it out of the hat also writes that storyteller's name down. Those two players won't get any credit, of course, but you never want to give away to anyone that you know the truth, so you must pretend to be thinking about your guess like everyone else, even if you know the truth. There's also the possibility that you will pick your own story out of the hat. In that case, you are the *only* player who really knows the truth when the stories are being told.

The next round begins as Player 2 announces the event she drew from the hat, and everyone (beginning with Player 3) pretends that this event happened to them as well. Players must do their best to convince everyone in the game that every single story they are telling is true—even though ultimately only one story from each player is factual. Go around the room telling stories for every event in the hat. Each time a player tells a story about an event, the other players should make notes as to who they believe and who they don't believe. After every player tells their story about the last event, all players come up with their final list of matches. Which event actually happened to each player? Once every player has their final answers clearly written next to each event on the numbered piece of paper, players reveal which story they told was actually true and the points are calculated.

Players receive 10 points for every story they match with the correct person. Players also receive 10 points for every player who *doesn't* guess their true story. In other words, players earn points for every player they fool!

For example, let's say the event Player 1 picked out was "Met Bill Murray." Player 2 must now pretend that it happened to her, even if it didn't. When Player 2 is done, Player 3 will do the same for the Bill Murray story. But in keeping with the three rules above, each player's response length will vary. Player 2 might say something like "I met Bill Murray four years ago in San Francisco with my friend Jack" and stop there. Player 3 might elaborate a bit more and say, "We were eating breakfast, and Bill came up to us and asked us how we liked our pancakes." Either way, it is your job to make people think it is actually your story if it isn't.

For scoring, let's say there are seven players in the example game above, that Player 5 really met Bill Murray, and Player 7 read the story. In this case, Player 5's and Player 7's votes won't count, because they already knew the answer, leaving five players to guess. (If Player 5 had read her own story, her vote would be the only one that didn't count.) If three players guessed Player 5, those three would each earn 10 points. Player 5 would receive 20 points (10 × the 2 players who guessed that it was someone else).

Important: The person who submitted an event must tell the truth about the story when it is his turn, but that player can still add some bluffing elements to his storytelling as long as everything he is saying is true. For example, that player might go on and on about the story, including true facts which seem ridiculous just to make people think he is lying. Sometimes, the person with the true story will hesitate on the facts just to make people believe he is putting too much thought into a fake story.

REVEALING YOUR HIDDEN TALENTS

PREPARATION:

Each player comes up with five things she is almost certain either nobody in the group is really great at, or that nobody in the group would ever brag about being great at. For example, you can submit normal things such as skiing, playing chess, or doing cartwheels, or you can submit silly or fun things, such as eating cake, writing the letter "C," playing with dirt, or juggling one banana. The sillier things tend to be more fun in this game. Either way, they can't be things you know you are good at (or anyone else in the group, for that matter). Players write the five items on separate pieces of paper and mix them in a hat or on the table with all the others.

OBJECTIVE:

Players must be the most convincing about their greatness in the skill they randomly select from the pile for most points.

GAME TIME:

Player 1 goes first and randomly selects an item from the pile. If it is something Player 1 submitted, she must put it back and pick again. In fewer than ten seconds, she must begin to make her case for how great she is at this skill. Player 1 wants to be as convincing as possible and really sell her greatness! She has sixty seconds. Next, Player 2 picks a random item and does the same. Every player repeats this process. Players don't have to take the full sixty seconds, but the more convincing arguments may take some time, especially for things that one wouldn't normally hear anyone brag about.

SCORING:

Once the last person argues his greatness, everyone votes for the two people they feel made the best arguments for the skills they selected. Each player votes for two other players. You cannot vote for your own. Write the two names on a piece of paper and give it to Player 1. Player 1 will tally the votes. Each player receives 1 point per vote. Play as many rounds as you like and declare a winner.

FOOL ME ONCE

T hese games are all about deception and your ability to fool the other players into believing you didn't say, write, or draw what you really *did* say, write, or draw—and to do your best not to be fooled by everyone else!

WHO WROTE THAT?

4–7
PLAYERS

COME UP WITH A SENTENCE
NOBODY WOULD BELIEVE WAS
WRITTEN BY YOU!

FOOL ME ONCE

PREPARATION:

Players take a piece of paper, write their name at the top, and make a numbered list from one to however many players there are in the game. (For example, if there are six players, you should have numbers one through six written vertically down your paper, with enough room to write a sentence next to each number.)

Each player should tear or cut another piece of paper into equal-sized strips (one strip per player in the game) and place them in the middle for all players to use. This should provide enough paper strips to complete one round per player.

OBJECTIVE:

In each round, players must come up with a sentence that the other players in the game would think was written by someone else, and then figure out who wrote all of the other sentences!

Players take turns coming up with an object or person to write about. It can be anything: a bar of soap, a pumpkin, an iguana, earwax, cousin Gretchen, etcetera. The player who chooses the subject announces it to the group. Each player must then come up with a sentence between five and ten words about that chosen subject and write it on one of the strips of paper. The sentence doesn't have to be true or make any sense whatsoever!

Important: Make sure your sentence is completely legible! It is advised to not write in cursive. Perhaps even write in block letters so not only is there no question anyone will be able to read it, but the person reading it won't be able to recognize the handwriting.

Each player must then fold his paper several times and place it in a hat or bowl mixed in with all of the other players' sentences. Each player then randomly picks out a sentence to read. (Players may even end up picking their own.)

Player 1 goes first and reads the sentence he picked out without making any gesture as to who he thinks wrote the sentence. That is sentence number one, and everyone writes it next to number one on their paper. Player 2 reads the next sentence, which is sentence number two, and everyone writes it next to number two on their paper. Play continues as the remaining players read the sentence they picked out until all sentences are read and written down.

Important: When you are reading a sentence, you don't want to give away who you think wrote it if, for instance, you recognize the handwriting, or you just know someone really well. You want to be the only one to guess correctly and get the points.

FOOL ME ONCE

Each player must now write down the name of the person they think wrote each sentence next to the sentence on the page. Players should circle their own name so the person scoring the answers knows not to give credit for that sentence. Once everyone is done placing an author next to each sentence, players pass their score sheets to the left. That player will score the sheet.

Once the sheets have been passed, the author of each sentence is revealed one at a time and points are tallied.

Player 2 now comes up with a subject to write about to play a second round.

Players earn 10 points for every answer they match with the right player (your own sentence doesn't count, of course) and 5 points for every player who didn't guess which sentence was theirs. The player with the most points after each round wins. Alternatively, keep track of the scores for each round for a grand total at the end.

EXAMPLE:

For example, let's say there are six players in the game. Player 1 selects "Uncle Mike" as his topic, so all players (including Player 1) write a sentence that is either about Uncle Mike or that includes Uncle Mike, and they place it in the hat. All players then choose a sentence from the hat, and the game begins.

After all the guesses have been written down and the sheets passed to the left, it is time to find out who wrote each sentence. Player 1 goes first and reads the sentence he picked out of the hat: "Uncle Mike has a big, fancy car." Player 2 reveals that she is the author. Points are awarded to players who got it right. If three players (other than Player 2) guessed correctly, those three players each earn 10 points and Player 2 earns 10 points (5 × 2) for the two other players who were fooled.

Player 2 then reads the next sentence, and Player 5 reveals that he is the author. Nobody guessed that he was the author, so Player 5 gets 25 points (5 × 5).

1) My pumpkin ate my dog.

_____

2) Pumpkin is best when served on a stick.

_____

3) My pumpkin looks like uncle Jack.

_____

4) Never take pumpkin on a road trip.

_____

5) I always said Levon is half man, half pumpkin.

_____

6) Patty Pumpkin played with Peter.

_____

7) Clearly Phil ate way too much pumpkin last night.

WHO DIDN'T WRITE THAT?

4-7 PLAYERS

//

FOOL ME ONCE

PREPARATION:

Players take a piece of paper, write their name at the top, and make a numbered list from one to however many players there are in the game. (For example, if there are six players, you should have numbers one through six written vertically down your paper with enough room to write a sentence next to each number.)

Each player should tear or cut another piece of paper into equal-size strips (one strip per player in the game) and place them in the middle for all players to use. This should provide enough paper strips to complete one round per player.

OBJECTIVE:

Each player tries to write something that is typically something she would write and obvious to everyone that she wrote it. The player who comes up with the subject substitutes her own sentence for one of the other player's sentences, and everyone has to figure out which sentence was substituted.

Starting with Player 1, players take turns coming up with an object or person to write about. Player 1 comes up with a subject. Everyone writes a sentence (five to ten words) on the subject, labeled with their name, and hands it to Player 1. After reading the sentences, Player 1 chooses one to discard and replace with a sentence she wrote. She then writes the name of the person she substituted her sentence for on the substituted sentence paper.

Note: The player coming up with the subject and reading the sentences should try to write a sentence which most people would believe was definitely written by the person she is choosing for the substitution.

Player 1 reads the adjusted set of sentences aloud in a random order, along with the name of the player who wrote each sentence (replacing her own name with that of the player whose sentence she replaced). She announces the name of each player by saying, "Bob wrote . . ." "Laura wrote . . ." or something similar.

Note: Player 1 doesn't associate her name with any sentence because she is pretending one of the other players wrote her sentence. Therefore, if there are seven total players in the game, Player 1 will read only six sentences, each one associated with another one of the other six players in the game.

Once Player 1 is done reading all the sentences, the other players must figure out which of the sentences was substituted. Everyone writes down the name of the person whose sentence they feel was substituted, and when pens are down, the guesses are revealed.

SCORING:

The player who comes up with the subject and is responsible for substituting a sentence earns 5 points for every player who didn't figure it out and was fooled. The player whose sentence was substituted also earns 5 points for every player who guessed wrong! Therefore, that player *must* not give away that his sentence was substituted when he first hears it!

Each player who guesses the substituted sentence correctly earns 5 points. Remember, the substituted player's vote won't count here—he earns points in a different way.

Finally, the players who didn't have their sentences substituted lose 5 points for each player who guessed it was theirs!

EXAMPLE:

Let's say, in a game with five players, Player 1 substituted her sentence for Player 2's. All the players write down their guesses and then reveal them. One player guessed correctly that Player 2's sentence had been substituted by Player 1. Two players guessed (incorrectly) that Player 3's sentence was substituted. Player 1 does not guess, and Player 2 already knows the answer, so scoring begins. Player 1 and Player 2 both earn 10 points, because they fooled two players. The player who guessed correctly earns 5 points. Player 3 loses 10 points because her sentence was selected by two other players.

It is obviously important in this game to write a sentence that is typical of something you would say so everyone thinks it was you! You don't want people thinking yours was substituted if it wasn't. In addition, when your sentence is substituted, you must do your best to pretend it was you and not be shocked when you hear a different sentence with you as the author. You earn the same amount of points as the person who substituted yours with hers. When you are responsible for selecting a person's sentence to substitute, you want to write a sentence that would more easily be recognized as something that person would write—even more than the sentence that person originally wrote.

FOOL ME ONCE

STORYTELLERS

///

HAVING TOO MUCH FUN MAKING UP STORIES!

PREPARATION:

Each player must come up with two fun events he wants other players to talk about as if they really happened. (For example, an event such as "I was attacked by a pack of angry squirrels in the Grand Canyon, but luckily was rescued by a supermodel in a golf cart," or, "I was on a long flight to Hong Kong and the guy next to me just kept slapping me in the face every thirty minutes for no reason," or, "I was with the president the other day and a talking kangaroo came over and peed on our breakfast." You get the picture.)

Every player writes the two events legibly on separate pieces of paper and then crumples each piece in a ball and places it in a hat, or mixed up on the table with all of the others.

OBJECTIVE:

Players must each talk about three strange events as if they really happened in their lives, using two events they pick from the hat and adding one of their own, without giving away which event is the one they added. Guessers must figure out which two events were picked from the pile and which one was added.

Player 1 goes first and picks two random events from the hat, without showing anyone what he picked. If he picks one of his own, he must put that one back, mix it back up in the hat, and pick another. Then Player 2 picks two random events from the hat. Again, if any event she picks is her own submission, she must put it back and pick again. Every player in the game follows the same process until the last player. The last player picks out the final two events. If either one of them belongs to her, she must toss the event away and ask each player in the game to come up with another event, crumple it up, and throw it in the pile. The last player will then pick again. This ensures that nobody tells a story that incorporates an event he submitted at the beginning.

In this game, a complete story for each player consists of three events. So, before Player 1 begins the storytelling, players take two minutes to decide what made-up event they wish to add to their story. The object is to make people believe this event was provided by someone else in the game. Players write down their third event on a separate piece of paper so they are ready to go with all three when it is their turn.

When Player 1 begins telling his story about three random events that happened in his life, he can begin with any of the three events and tell them in any order. It is fun when everyone starts their storytelling by saying something like, "Did I ever tell you guys about the time I . . . ?" Then, after talking about the first event, players can say, "Oh, and then there was that time I . . ." and continue with the second event, and so on.

Players can also ad lib as much as they want with each of the three events. That's another element that makes the storytelling so much fun.

After Player 1 is done telling his complete story about all three memorable events in his life, he then asks the rest of the players, "Which of these events did I add myself?" To make it clear, Player 1 numbers each of the events that he told. The rest of the players must decide which event Player 1 added himself. Players write down their guesses, and on the count of three, the guesses are all revealed at once.

Every player goes around the room telling fun stories while also trying to disguise his added event.

EXAMPLE:

Using the above sample events, let's say Player 1 picked out the following two events from the hat:

1. "I was attacked by a pack of angry squirrels in the Grand Canyon but was luckily rescued by a supermodel in a golf cart."

2. "I was on a long flight to Hong Kong and the guy next to me just kept slapping me in the face every thirty minutes for no reason."

Player 1 will now have to add another event to talk about. For example, he may add, "My grandmother was a champion yogurt wrestler and always made the family wrestle in different flavored yogurts every Friday night."

SCORING:

For every story, guessing players each earn 5 points if they guess the added story correctly. The storyteller earns 3 points for every player who gets it wrong.

Every time one of your submitted events is in another player's story, you have a fifty-fifty chance of guessing correctly. If you were lucky enough to have one player pick out both of your events, you will win easy points for that player's story.

WHO DREW THAT?

HOW WELL CAN YOU DISGUISE YOUR ARTISTIC TALENTS?

PREPARATION:

Players take turns coming up with an interesting object for the group to draw (e.g., a haunted house, an upside-down car, a bird with gigantic eyes, a gorilla on roller skates, etc.). The object doesn't have to be simple; it can be fun, silly, and even complicated.

> **Important:** Players should all use the exact same color and type of writing instruments (e.g., all pencils or all blue pens). And do not let anyone see what you are drawing!

OBJECTIVE:

Players must attempt to disguise their own drawing style and determine who drew all of the other pictures.

GAME TIME:

Starting with Player 1's object, every player must draw that same object. Allow up to two minutes for drawing time.

Note: You must make some real attempt at drawing a picture. You can't just draw a few lines, and no stick figures are allowed. Also, if your drawing skills are quite good or you have a specific style and everyone knows it, you may want to come up with a series of new drawing styles for this game!

When everyone is finished drawing, players place their completed pictures face-down at the center of the table. Player 1 mixes the pictures up and then turns them over, writing a number on the top of each picture clearly enough for everyone to see. Players must now determine who drew each picture. Players make their lists, which might look something like this:

Picture 1: John

Picture 2: Mary

Picture 3: Katherine (. . . and so on.)

Play continues, and players reveal their drawings, tally points, and then move on to the next player's object.

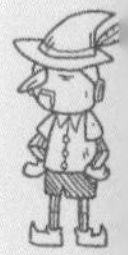

SCORING:

Players earn 1 point for every player they fool and 1 point for every picture they match correctly. Therefore, when the true artist is revealed for each picture, each player who got it right should raise her hand and give herself a point. The artist will then count the people who got it wrong and give himself that many points for fooling those people.

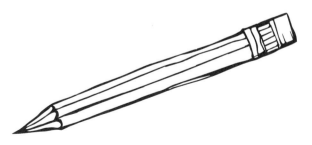

LEFT AND RIGHT

4+
PLAYERS

//

PREPARATION:

Players sit or stand in a circle.

OBJECTIVE:

One player in each round makes the ultimate decision on which two-word phrase to use and tries to fool others in the game, with help from the players on her left and right. Guessers do their best to figure it out!

GAME TIME:

Player 1 asks the player to the left and the player to the right, one at a time, to whisper a two-word phrase in her ear. (Any two words will do, and they don't have to actually go together or make any sense.)

Player 1 then decides if she is going to use one of their phrases or come up with one of her own.

Note: When you are sitting to the left or right of the player leading the round (Player 1 for the first round) and are being asked to come up with a two-word phrase, the key is to come up with two words nobody would ever think you said. At the same time, if Player 1

Once Player 1 makes the decision, she says the two-word phrase out loud to the rest of the players. The other players must now decide who came up with that phrase. Was it Player 1, or one of the players to her left or right? Everyone reveals their answer at once by pointing to the player they select, and all players tally their points. Play continues as Player 2 gets phrases from the players to his left and right, and so on.

SCORING:

Players earn points if they are able to fool the other players. The player who leads the round and the players to her left and right each get 1 point for every player who is fooled. It doesn't matter whether the phrase ultimately belongs to Player 1 or the player to either side—the three players are in this together and are scored together.

If a player guesses correctly, he earns 2 points.

So, if there are eight total players, three determine the two-word phrase (Player 1, Player 2 to his left, and Player 8 to his right, for example) and the other five would guess. Let's say Player 2's phrase is the one said aloud, and three players correctly guess Player 2, one incorrectly guesses Player 1, and one incorrectly guesses Player 8. The three players who guessed correctly earn 2 points each. Players 1, 2, and 8 each earn 2 points—one for each player who guessed incorrectly.

NEXT

Play rotates, with Player 2 making the decision and the players to his left and right offering the two-word phrase suggestions.

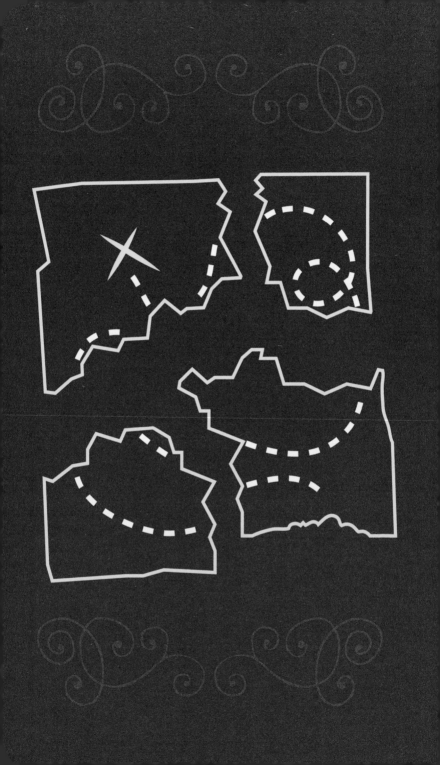

I hese games all require some sort of strategy that will enable you to have the best chance to win. For several of these games, the strategy is all about how you put together a specific challenge for the rest of the group when it is your turn. The scoring system is the driving force behind this strategy, as you determine how much of a risk you are willing to take while creating a fun and competitive experience for all.

THE NAME GAME

3+ PLAYERS

//

IT'S ALL ABOUT REACTIONS TO YOUR CLUES

PREPARATION:

Put all of the letters of the alphabet on small pieces of paper in a hat, leaving out Q, U, X, Y, and Z. Each player then picks out two letters and decides to keep one and put the other back. Now each player takes a little time to think of a well-known person they want to give clues about when their turn comes. That well-known person's first name must begin with the letter chosen. Write the name down on a piece of paper and place it face-down.

OBJECTIVE:

The ultimate goal is to give just enough clues to get everyone but one person to guess your famous person. Playing it safe will earn you points, but going too far will lead to disaster!

GAME TIME:

Player 1 begins. He shows the letter he picked and puts sixty seconds on the clock. Player 1 now starts to give clues to get people to guess his well-known person. Player 1 can give as many or few clues as he wants—completely up to him. It is truly about the reaction he is receiving when giving clues. The strategy is all about the scoring! When the sixty seconds are up, each player guessing must put his guess on a piece of paper within ten seconds and reveal it at the count of three. (Players can write their guess before the sixty seconds are up if they already know the answer.) Then scores are recorded.

SCORING:

Player 1 receives 1 point per player who guesses his person correctly. Every other player gets 2 points for guessing correctly. Here's the catch for Player 1: If nobody guesses your well-known name, you lose 1 point per person in the game. So, with eight total players, you lose 8 points if nobody guesses your name. In addition, if EVERYONE guesses your person, you get no points at all! This scoring system creates the need to get at least one person to figure it out and the temptation to get as many people as possible to guess without going too far.

> **Important:** You can give as many clues as you like, and you can say whatever you like. You can even wait until there are ten seconds left on the clock to start giving your first clue. However, even if you only give one clue at the beginning of your round and stop talking, all players get the full sixty seconds to try to figure it out. Nobody else should be talking once the timer starts, and everyone except Player 1 should remain silent until all guesses are made!

NEXT:

Player 2 reveals her letter and puts sixty seconds on the clock. After every player has taken a turn, letters are put back in the hat for a new series.

WHICH WORD SHOULD YOU HIDE?

PREPARATION:

Each player thinks of three two-word combinations like House Boat, Ear Wax, George Clooney, Jump Rope, and so on. Players will eventually be giving all three to the group, but they will only give the first letter of one of the words in each combination. The group will have to figure out the rest of the word. Therefore, when coming up with each combination, players will need to understand the game play and strategy.

OBJECTIVE:

Provide three two-word combinations that will lead to most people figuring them out—but not everyone!

GAME TIME:

Player 1 begins, giving her three two-word combinations to the group by saying one of the words and only the first letter of the other in each combination. For example, she may say "House B, J Rope, and George C." Or she can go with "H Boat, Jump R, and G Clooney"—any combination she feels will be just the right one to get most people to figure out all three, but *not everyone*! Once the combinations are given, the other players have sixty seconds to figure out the rest of the three words and write the answers down. Players must come up with all three words for credit! In the example with House B, J Rope, and George C, the answers would be Boat, Jump, and Clooney.

Once all guesses are made, Player 1 reveals the correct answers and points are handed out. Player 1 receives 2 points per player who guessed all three correctly. Every other player gets 2 points for guessing all three correctly. You must have *all three* correct. No partial credit!

Here's the catch for Player 1: If nobody guesses all three or if everyone guesses all three, you lose 1 point per every person in the game! So with eight total players, you lose 8 points if either nobody or everyone guesses all three words! This scoring system creates the need to get at least one person to figure out all three words, and the temptation to get as many people as possible to guess without going too far for maximum points on your turn.

Play continues with Player 2 giving his three to the group, and so on.

MAKE A PLAN, STAN!

ENTERTAINMENT BUFFS

COMBINING STRATEGY WITH DISCOVERY

PREPARATION:

Players decide on a category for their turn: movies, TV shows, or singers/groups.

OBJECTIVE:

To get one person to figure out the movie, show, or group selected based on the choices provided and just the right clue.

GAME TIME:

Player 1 will go first and give everyone his category. Each player must now announce a selection for that category one at a time, beginning with Player 2, and everyone writes them down. For example, if Player 1 says his category is "Movies," the other players will each pick a movie they think Player 1 knows and they know as well. If someone says a movie you wanted to give before it is your turn, then you must select a different one. Everyone writes them down as they are announced. (This game can be played with no writing as well, especially with few players.) After all movies are mentioned, Player 1 now has sixty seconds to give a clue or clues to the group about the movie he chose from the selections provided. The clues can be anything about the movie. However, Player 1 only wants *one person* to figure it out to get the maximum points, and he absolutely *needs* the player whose movie he chose to be that person. When playing with paper and pens, everyone writes down their guess after sixty seconds and places it face-down on the table, revealing their guesses at the count of three. With no writing, numbers are assigned in order around the table for each movie, and at the count of three, everyone holds up the number of fingers associated with their guess.

SCORING:

Each player who guesses correctly receives 25 points. Player 1 receives 100 points if the player who submitted the movie is the *only* one who guessed correctly. Player 1 receives 50 points if two players guessed correctly, including the player who submitted the movie. Player 1 receives 0 points if more than two people guessed correctly. In addition, Player 1 loses 50 points if the player who submitted the movie doesn't get it right, regardless of how many other people guessed it. Finally, if nobody or everybody gets it, Player 1 loses 100 points! Therefore, your highest priority is to get the player who submitted the movie to get it right! Then you want as few other people to guess it, preferably nobody else for the 100 points.

NEXT:

Play continues with Player 2 giving her category to the group and, beginning with Player 3, everyone offers options.

GOTCHA!

FIGURE OUT WHAT THEY ARE
GOING TO SPELL AND SPOIL
THEIR FUN!

PREPARATION:

Write all the letters of the alphabet on separate pieces of paper. Mix them up and place them face-down on a table or in a hat where nobody can see them. (You may want to consider leaving out Q, X, and Z.)

OBJECTIVE:

Players take turns pairing up to try to spell words together, without either player knowing in advance what word they are going to spell.

GAME TIME:

Player 1 picks a letter out of the hat. Players 1 and 2 now take turns spelling a word, one letter at a time, beginning with the letter Player 1 picked out of the hat. (No names or "-s" plurals allowed!) Player 2 now says one random letter. Player 1 says a random letter, and Player 2 says a fourth letter. After four letters, the game is put on pause and the rest of the players in the game must guess what word Players 1 and 2 are going to spell. Each player writes her guess on a piece of paper and places it face-down in the center of the table with her name on it.

Then Players 1 and 2 continue spelling their word, all the time never communicating with each other. Players 1 and 2 should never talk other than to exchange letters. Once Player 1 or Player 2 thinks they are done spelling the word, that player says "Stop." Either player can say "Stop" at any time. At that point, all players turn over their guesses to see if anyone was correct, and points are awarded.

Play continues when Player 3 draws a new first letter, and Players 3 and 4 take turns trying to spell a new word. Change up the pairings on each round.

SCORING:

If at least one player guessed the word correctly, that player and anyone else who guessed the word earns 50 points, and Players 1 and 2 lose 50 points each! The other players in the game get no points.

However, if nobody guessed the word, Players 1 and 2 multiply the number of letters in their word by 10, and that is how many points they each earn. Nobody else loses or earns any points.

Important: If the two players misspell a word, they each lose ten times the number of letters in the word they created, and everyone else in the game earns 25 points.

In addition, if Player 1 or Player 2 thinks at any time while spelling that they are in danger of not spelling a word at all or spelling one incorrectly, the player should say "Stop!" immediately. In this case, multiply the number of letters already used in the incomplete word by 10, and that is how many points Players 1 and 2 each lose in that round. Everyone else in the game earns 25 points each.

If the letter picked out of the hat by Player 1 is R, and the next three letters Player 1 and Player 2 choose brought the word to REPU, then some possible guesses could include "republic," "reputable," "repugnant," "reputation," and so on. (Remember, "-s" plurals of words are not allowed. This rule exists to keep players from slapping an extra "s" on the end of a word for more points. Plurals such as "people," "teeth," etc. would be acceptable, while "dogs" or "republics" would not.)

If the word ended up being "reputation" and nobody guessed it, the total points for Players 1 and 2 would be 100 (10 × 10). However, if one person got it right, that person would earn 50 points, and Players 1 and 2 would each lose 50 points!

SPELLING BEE

4+ PLAYERS

THE ULTIMATE CREATIVE SPELLING CONTEST

PREPARATION:

Players take turns coming up with a made-up word, such as "scratchamytoesis" or "flabborizer" or "juicetastible."

OBJECTIVE:

Players make up a word and try to trick the other players into spelling it incorrectly.

GAME TIME:

Player 1 begins by writing down her word without letting anyone see, then pronounces it aloud to the group. She places the correct spelling face-down on the table with her name on it. Each player then writes down what she thinks is the correct spelling of that word and puts her pen down when ready. One by one, each player reveals her guess.

Tip: Players may ask for the part of speech or to hear the word in a sentence, and the player who provided the word must oblige.

SCORING:

Each player who spells the word correctly earns 20 points. The creator of the word earns 10 points for each player who gets it wrong, with one important exception: if nobody spells the word correctly, Player 1 loses 50 points for that round and every other player earns 10 points.

Tip: Make your word hard, but not too hard! In this game, you want only one person to get it right to earn the maximum amount of points for your word.

THREE OF A KIND

5+ PLAYERS

INDEX CARDS RECOMMENDED

> ## BE THE ONLY ONE TO FIND THE THREE ITEMS THAT GO TOGETHER!

PREPARATION:

To start, everyone needs to write down three related words or items; for example, rye, wheat, and white (breads); rabbit, fish, and bird (pets); scream, dream, and steam (words that rhyme); Goofy, Pluto, and Donald Duck (Disney characters); or DeNiro, Redford, and Pattinson (all Roberts). Players write these three-of-a-kind words on three separate index cards without letting the other players see what they have written.

> **Note:** Be creative, but keep in mind that you don't want to make your three too easy or too difficult for people to figure out.

As the other players are writing down three items for the first round, the first player to finish must also create "Bluff Cards." A Bluff Card is an index card with the word "Bluff" written on it, and these same cards can be used for all subsequent rounds. To determine the number of Bluff Cards needed, take the total number of players in the game and subtract 3. (For example, if you have seven players in the game, you will need four Bluff Cards.) Make sure players write lightly on the index cards with pens or pencils, so the words won't show through on the other side.

OBJECTIVE:

In this game, players need to use their best bluffing skills! Players try to fool everyone else into thinking they drew a different card than the one they actually drew while trying to guess the real "three-of-a-kind" match. The fewer players who guess the real three-of-a-kind correctly, the more points those players receive.

GAME TIME:

Player 1 holds on to one of his three index cards and mixes the other two with all of the Bluff Cards, face-down so no one can see them. Then he asks each player, starting with the player to his left, to randomly draw a card without revealing to anyone which card he picked. Once a player sees what is written on the chosen card, he hides it until later.

Players who draw a Bluff Card must try to make people believe they picked one of Player 1's three-of-a-kind set. Players who drew one of the three-of-a-kind cards must say the word on the card when it is their turn; the catch is that these players want to make the rest of the players think they are bluffing.

Player 1 goes first and says the word on the card he held back for himself. Player 2 then says a related word. If Player 2 drew one of Player 1's three-of-a-kind cards, she must say that word; if she drew a Bluff Card, she must try to convince the other players that whatever word she makes up is the real match to Player 1's word.

Important: If a person with a Bluff Card says one of the two real words in the three-of-a-kind set before the person who actually has the word gets to say it, the roles reverse, and the person who actually has the word *must now bluff and come up with something else to make people choose his new word as part of the three-of-a kind group.*

Players who happen to select one of the three-of-a-kind cards at the beginning have a major advantage because they already know two of the words; they only need to guess the third.

After every player in the game has had the chance to bluff or say the word on his card, each player must write down his guess for which three items were Player 1's three-of-a-kind set. Once all of the guesses are written down, it's pens down! Players cannot change their guesses during the reveal.

Once the scores are tallied, Player 2 begins a new round with her three-of-a-kind set, and play continues until all players have had the chance to lead a round.

SCORING:

For the players who guessed correctly, the amount of points they each receive is equivalent to ten times the number of people who got it wrong! (For example, with six players in the game, if four got it wrong and two got it right, those two players who got it right would each earn 40 points. Remember, Player 1 will not guess.) The players who got it wrong don't earn any points.

The player who created the three-of-a-kind set earns 50 points if:

1. at least one person gets it right, and
2. no more than half of the guessers get it right.

If more than half of the players get it right, Player 1 gets no points at all. In addition—and this is important—if either nobody or everybody guesses correctly, Player 1 loses 20 points and every other player in the game earns 20 points.

This point system is put in place to make sure everyone tries their hardest to fool everyone else and to encourage players to make their three-of-a-kind set challenging, but not too challenging.

EXAMPLE:

Using one of the examples above (pets: rabbit, fish, and bird), let's say Player 1 kept "fish" for himself and mixed "rabbit" and "bird" in with the Bluff Cards. Player 1 starts by simply saying, "Fish." Now Player 2 has to say a word. Player 2 drew a Bluff Card; now she must say something that she believes goes with "fish" so everyone thinks her word is part of the three-of-a-kind set. She decides to say, "Shark." Now it's Player 3's turn. If Player 3 drew the "rabbit" card, he must say, "Rabbit," but he can hesitate to make people think he has a Bluff Card.

Let's say Player 5 drew the "bird" card, but before he has the chance to use it, Player 4 bluffs and says, "Bird." Player 5 must now think of something else to make everyone think he has one of the three-of-a-kind cards. Additionally, Player 5 now knows that Player 4 drew one of the Bluff Cards, but Player 4 doesn't necessarily know that she came up with one of the real three-of-a-kind items when she was bluffing. This makes for an interesting set of circumstances, and the bluffs—and the stakes—build.

For scoring, let's say there are seven players in the above example with pets. After every player takes a turn, everyone except Player 1 writes down their guesses for what they think are the real three of a kind. If two of the six players guessing get it right, those two players earn 40 points (10 times the four players who guessed incorrectly). The four who were wrong do not earn any points. Player 1 earns 50 points because at least one person got it right and no more than half got it right. However, if four of the six players guessing got it right, then those four players would each earn 20 points (10 times the two players who guessed incorrectly) and Player 1 would not earn any points, since more than half of the players guessing got it right. Essentially, the three of a kind was too easy. Keep in mind, though, if everyone or nobody guesses correctly, Player 1 loses 20 points and everyone else gets 20.

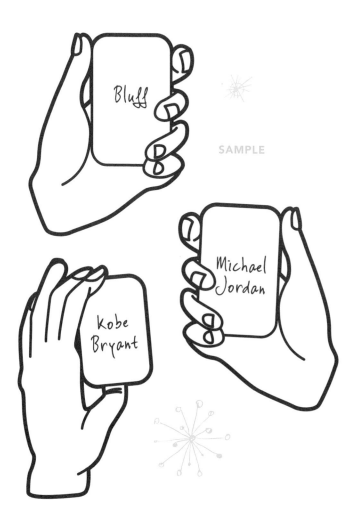

SAMPLE

WHO IS IT?

3+
PLAYERS

ALL ABOUT THE LAST CLUE

PREPARATION:

Players decide on a category for their turn. Select either Movies/TV/Books, Music, Sports, or History/Science/Politics. Then they decide on a person they want people to try to guess in their category. Write that person's name down without letting anyone see! The first name and last name are combined in one long list of letters on top of blanks. For example, Marlon Brando should be written like this: M a r l o n B r a n d o.

OBJECTIVE:

To get at least one person to figure out the name for points. Nobody right or everyone right earns nothing!

GAME TIME:

Player 1 goes first and announces the category, then provides the total number of letters in the person's first and last name when combined and written together. (For Marlon Brando, the total number of letters is twelve.) Everyone writes down that number of blanks. Player 1 does not say how many letters are in the first or last name specifically. Next, Player 1 will begin with the first of three total clues. Player 1 gives the first

clue, which is the first letter of the first name and the last letter of the last name. Everyone writes them down on the first
and last blanks on their pages. Sixty seconds on the clock! If a
player thinks she knows who it is after the first clue, she fills in
the blanks on his paper without letting anyone see, turns her
page over, and writes the number 25 on the back. Those people who guessed after the first clue must stay silent! When
sixty seconds are up after the first clue, Player 1 gives the
second clue, which is the second letter in the first name and
the second-to-last letter in the last name. Sixty seconds on
the clock. Again, the people who think they have the name
figured out after the second clue fill it in without letting anyone see, turn their pages over, and this time write the number
10 on the back. Those people as well must now stay silent
for the rest of the round. The final clue is completely up to
Player 1. Player 1 will provide two more letters, but they can
be anywhere on the blanks. This is a strategy play based on
what has happened thus far and the scoring system. After the
third clue is provided, another sixty seconds are placed on
the clock for the remaining players. Final guesses are made
by those players if they think they have it, and they turn their
papers over. Those final guessers after the third clue write the
number 5 on the back. If players still don't have a guess after
the third clue, they can just leave their page blank. No need
to turn it over and no points for this round. Player 1 will then
ask the 25-point players (who guessed after the first clue) to
reveal their guesses. Then she will ask the 10-point players
(who guessed after the second clue), and then the 5-point
players. Player 1 will then turn over her page and reveal the
correct answer.

SCORING:

Every player who answered correctly after the first clue gets 25
points. Every player who answered correctly after the second

clue gets 10 points. Every player who answered correctly after the third clue gets 5 points. There is one exception: if you are the only one in the game to get the answer right after the second or third clue, you get a full 25 points, not 5 or 10!

The player coming up with the name (in this case Player 1) gets 25 points *only* if at least one person figures it out after three clues, but *not everyone*. If either nobody or everybody figures out the person, Player 1 gets no points. So, for the third clue strategy; if Player 1 is pretty certain that at least one person has already figured it out before the third clue, she will make the third clue letters as difficult as possible. On the other hand, if she sees that nobody has turned their papers over with guesses before the third clue, she may provide a relatively easy clue so that at least one person figures it out!

NEXT:

Play continues with Player 2 giving his category to the group, the number of letters, and the first and last letters of the combined first and last names for the first clue.

FIRST AND LAST

3+ PLAYERS

FIND THE RIGHT MIX
FOR YOUR GROUP

PREPARATION:

Each player must come up with four words that each have the same first and last letter. For example: Market, Meat, Merchant, Malevolent. All four begin with "M" and end with "T." Write them all down on a piece of paper without letting anyone see, and note how many letters are in each word to the right of each word.

OBJECTIVE:

For maximum points, players want to get as many people as possible to guess each of their four words—without everyone getting it right! The longer the words, the more points everyone receives. The player creating the words stands to receive the most points, but also takes on all the risk.

GAME TIME:

Player 1 starts by letting everyone know the first and last letters of each of his four words. Using the example in the Preparation section, he would say, "For my four words, the beginning letter is 'M' and the last letter is 'T.'" Player 1 then tells everyone how many letters are in each of the four words. Again, using the example above, he would say, "The first word is six letters, second word is four letters, third word is eight letters, and the last word is ten letters." While Player 1 is giving the total number of letters in each word, all of the players are writing blanks on their pieces of paper for each word, with "M" over the first blank of each and "T" over the last blank of each. Finally, Player 1 will decide if he wants to give away any more letters in any of the words. The strategy is all based on the scoring system, so it is completely up to Player 1 how many more letter clues he wants to give, if any. For example, after giving the number of letters in all four words, Player 1 might say, "Also, the third letter of the last word is 'L,' the third letter of the eight-letter word is 'R,' and the fifth letter of that same word is 'H.'" Once Player 1 is done giving clues, he makes that claim and sets a timer for three minutes, and all players begin searching for the answers. Once three minutes are up, players pass their completed pages to the right for the player next to them to score their card. Player 1 then reveals the correct answers.

SCORING FOR PLAYERS GUESSING:

For every word you get right, you get the points equivalent to the number of letters in the word. So, for the word "Meat," you get 4 points. For the word "Market," you get 6 points. For the word "Merchant," you get 8 points, and for the word "Malevolent," you get 10 points.

SCORING FOR THE PLAYERS PROVIDING THE CHALLENGE:

For each of your words, your points are equivalent to the number of letters in the word plus the number of people who got it right. So, for a six-letter word, if three people out of four get it right, you get 9 points. (6 letters in the word + 3 people who found the word.) Or, for a ten-letter word with two people finding the word, you get 12 points. (10-letter word + 2 people.)

There are, however, two major scoring exceptions in this game. If everyone gets your word right, you get no points for that word. In addition, for any of your four words that *nobody* guesses, you get no points and everyone else in the game gets 5 points.

NEXT:

Play continues with Player 2 providing the first and last letters of her four words, the number of letters in each, and any specific additional letters she wants to offer up—if any.

FOUR OF A KIND

4+
PLAYERS

FIND A COMMON THEME!

PREPARATION:

None. This game can be played with or without paper and pens.

OBJECTIVE:

Players come up with a "Four-of-a-Kind" where the final clue will be enough for most to read their mind, but not everyone—and figure out the other puzzles from the other players for maximum points!

GAME TIME:

Each player thinks of a "Four-of-a-Kind." These are four words that go together in some way. For example:

- Basketball, baseball, football, and hockey—all sports
- Peas, carrots, broccoli, corn—all vegetables
- Toyota, Honda, Ford, Chevrolet—all automobile manufacturers

The "Four-of-a-Kind" can be any four words that go together. How *well* they go together doesn't matter; there is no right answer. It is all about whether people will be able to figure it out and how many will do so.

Next, each player determines which of the four words will be the one every other player must figure out. That word will only be known in the puzzle by its first letter, and everyone must try to figure out the word.

For example, Player 1 goes first and decides to go with the vegetable example above. She determines that "Corn" is the word she wants to hide. She says to the group: "Broccoli, Carrots, Peas, and 'C'." Once she does this, sixty seconds go on the clock for every other player to figure out what the "C" stands for. When playing with pens and paper, each player will write down a guess before the time is up, and all players will reveal their guesses at once. Player 1 will have also written down the correct answer before the timer had begun so she can turn it over once everyone reveals their guesses. With no pens and paper, players are all on the honor system and everyone will reveal one at a time what they had for "C," if they had anything at all. Player 1 then reveals who was right.

SCORING:

Each player gets 2 points if they guessed right and no points for guessing wrong. Simple enough. However, Player 1 gets 2 points for every person who guessed right, with two exceptions! First, if everyone gets it right, Player 1 loses 2 points, and everyone else keeps their 2 points. Second, if nobody gets it right, Player 1 loses 2 points and everyone else in the game gets 2 points. Therefore, in either of these scenarios, Player 1 will be on the wrong end of a four-point swing—everyone will get 2 and she will lose 2.

STRATEGY:

Given what you just read in the scoring section, the strategy in this game is to come up with three items and a letter for the fourth that won't be too obvious and also won't be too difficult! The trick is to make sure at least one person gets it and at least one person doesn't. It really also comes down to how much of a risk you are willing to take. For example, if your group is full of people who know the Beatles at least fairly well, it probably wouldn't be a wise move for your "Four-of-a-Kind" puzzle to be, "John, Paul, George, R." Chances are everyone will get Ringo and that will be a fail. On the other hand, if you have someone in the room you know doesn't even know the Beatles at all, or perhaps won't be able to come up with it in sixty seconds, it may be worth the risk!

NEXT:

Player 2 gives his "Four-of-a-Kind," and so on. Play as many rounds as you like, but make sure each player has the same number of turns offering up a challenge.

FOUR-LETTER ILLUSTRATIONS

> ## MAY THE ARTISTIC FORCE BE WITH YOU

PREPARATION:

Each player submits ten different four-letter words on separate pieces of paper to the hat, or face-down on the table mixed with all the others. Any four-letter words will do. Players also prepare a big piece of paper with their name on it for drawings. Divide the paper into a grid of four quadrants, each for a separate drawing. Finally, players take a separate piece of paper and write everyone's name on it, including their own, down the left-hand side. This will be used for guesses and scoring.

OBJECTIVE:

Artists do their absolute best to communicate their four-letter word through their four drawings in the time allotted. Guessers try to figure out each of the four-letter words based on their best interpretation of what they see.

GAME TIME:

Each player picks one paper or card from the mixed-up pile of four-letter words without showing anyone what he picked.

He must now try to communicate his four-letter word to the group by drawing four different pictures on his paper, which is separated into a grid of four quadrants. The first letter of the *subject* of each drawing is one of the letters in the four-letter word.

For example: If the four-letter word you pick is "Rock," you must place a drawing in the upper-left corner of your grid where the subject begins with the letter "R." Perhaps you can draw a rainbow, or rain, or a rock-et—whatever you can draw best that will most clearly be identified, therefore telling people the first letter of your word begins with an "R." The drawing for the second letter of your word must go in the upper-right corner. In this case, you can draw an orange, oval, owl, octopus, or anything else that starts with "O." The drawing for the third letter of your word goes in the bottom-left corner, and the drawing for the fourth letter goes in the bottom-right corner.

Let's say for the word "Rock," Player 1 drew a rocket, an owl, a car, and a king. If those drawings were clear enough to the other players, they should have all been able to identify Player 1's four-letter word. Players have five minutes on the clock to perfect their drawings before pens are put down. There can be no letters or numbers on any of the drawings. In addition, players may not draw the same picture if they play multiple rounds of this game. So, if you draw a car for the "C" in the word "Rock" in round one, and then your next word in round two is "Crop," you would not be able to draw another car or rocket or owl for "Crop." Once the five minutes are up, pens go down and players turn their papers over. Now every player gets the card or paper with all the player's names. That is where they will write their guesses.

At the count of three, each player passes their drawing to the right and everyone has a maximum of sixty seconds to figure out the four-letter word and write it next to the player's name on their card. When sixty seconds are up, pages must be turned over. Players then pass the next paper with drawings to the right again and repeat, with sixty seconds on the clock. Do this until everyone has their original drawing back, and scoring will begin.

SCORING:

Pass your paper with the guesses to the person next to you. That person will score your guesses. Player 1 begins by turning his page over for everyone to see and announcing what his four-letter word is, and others can congratulate him or question his fine drawing. Players raise their hands if the card in front of them has the correct guess. Each player who guessed correctly gets 1 point. The scorers will note the point next to the guess on the card they are scoring. In addition, Player 1 gets a point for every player who guessed his exact four-letter word. The player who has his card will put the number of points he got from the guessers next to his name on his card. Player 2 then reveals her four-letter word, scorers note if the player whose card they are scoring got it right, and Player 2's scorer notes how many people got hers right and records that number next to Player 2's name on the card, and so on.

NEXT:

Continue to play as many rounds as you like, but keep in mind that nobody can draw the same picture twice—no matter how many rounds you play.

RISK IT OR NOT!

TAKE A RISK WITH A FEW BIG
WORDS OR BE CONSERVATIVE
WITH MANY SMALL WORDS

PREPARATION:

Every player draws twenty-five blanks in one long line.

OBJECTIVE:

The objective is to spell words over the twenty-five blanks, using the letters provided by all of the players until all twenty-five blanks are used. The longer each word is in each player's string, the more points she gets.

GAME TIME:

Starting with Player 1 and going clockwise around the table, each player says one random letter, and everyone must put that letter on one of the twenty-five blanks. Letters do not have to be placed in the order they're announced, but once placed in a slot, that letter cannot be moved, so strategize before writing a letter down. Continue going around the circle saying letters until all twenty-five slots are filled. Letters can be repeated.

In each round, a different player should go first. To give every player a chance to go first, the number of rounds played should be equal to the number of players in the game.

SCORING:

The number of letters in a word multiplied by itself is the number of points you get for that word.

EXAMPLE:

Once all twenty-five letters are chosen, a final game board for Player 1 might look like this:

FRIENDAJPLOWLEKCRAMPEDSSA

Player 1 earns 36 points for "Friend" (6 × 6), 16 points for "Plow" (4 × 4), and 49 points for "Cramped" (7 × 7), for a total of 101 points.

Player 2's game board in the same round (using the same letters) might look like this:

PAMPERDRJAWAKENCDFLOSSEIL

Player 2 earns 36 points for "Pamper" (6 × 6), 36 points for "Awaken" (6 × 6), and 25 points for "Floss" (5 × 5), for a total of 97 points.

WORD NERD BONUS SCORING:

In this version, players can strategize to overlap words in order to get the most points out of their letters. In addition, words within words count as well. Scoring follows the same principles as regular play—the number of letters in a word squared. For example, the word "Friend" would still be worth 36 points (6 × 6), but clever players would also see the word "End" in "Friend" and add an additional 9 points (3 × 3). The same would be true of "Cramped" (7 × 7 for 49) and "Amped" (5 × 5 for an additional 25).

WHO AM I?

4+
PLAYERS

INDEX CARDS
RECOMMENDED

//

GET EVERYONE TO GUESS YOUR LIST OF FAMOUS PEOPLE IN AS FEW CLUES AS POSSIBLE

PREPARATION:

Each player makes a list of twenty famous people (no fictional or animated characters allowed) and writes each of them on individual pieces of paper with his own name underneath each one. These are the game pieces, which are all mixed up in a hat or other object to prevent anyone from seeing them.

OBJECTIVE:

Players must try to get all of the other players in the game to guess their "famous person" picks in as few clues as possible—preferably just one!

GAME TIME:

Player 1 goes first and picks pieces out of the hat without looking or letting anyone else see who he picked. The number of pieces chosen is equivalent to the number of players in the game, minus the player who draws the pieces. (For example, if there are seven players in the game, Player 1 draws six pieces.)

Player 1 must now try to get all of the other players in the game to guess one of the famous people he picked using only one-word clues and a maximum of three clues per name. Here's the catch: Player 1 must assign each famous person to *one specific* player to guess.

Player 1 can assign the famous people he drew to whichever players he wants, with one exception: he may not ask a player to guess one of the famous people she submitted to the pile. (That is why everyone puts their names underneath each famous person they submit.)

Tip: The player giving the clues should determine which player is most likely to guess each famous person based on his or her interests.

Player 1 selects the player he wants to have guess his first famous person and gives the first clue. Players can use one-word clues *only*, and no clue can be any part of the person's name. (For example, if you want someone to guess "Sylvester Stallone," your first clue could be "Rocky." If you want someone to say "Marlon Brando," your first clue could be "Godfather.") Player 1 tries to get players to guess their assigned famous person one at a time. He will try to get Player 2 to guess her assigned person in one clue, adding a second or third clue if necessary, and then move on to Player 3.

Each player in the game must have the chance to attempt to guess one of the selections. Players may not skip anyone or use a player twice. Each player in the game has no more than thirty seconds after each clue. Once Player 1 has either succeeded or failed to elicit correct guesses from each of the other players, play continues with Player 2, who draws the same number of names from the hat and assigns them to the other players to guess.

Note: Once a game piece is used, it must be tossed away. Also, if a famous person is selected from the hat

SCORING:

If the player who Player 1 selected to guess a name guesses correctly with just one clue, both players earn 3 points. If the player guesses in two clues, both players earn 2 points. In three clues, both players earn 1 point each. If a player doesn't guess correctly in three clues, neither player (the guesser or the clue giver) gets any points, and Player 1 moves on to the next player with a new name. For example, if there are five total players in the game, you can earn a maximum of 12 points (3 × 4 four players) each time it is your turn to pick the game pieces and give clues.

EXAMPLE:

There are five total players, so Player 1 draws four names out of the hat. The names are: "Robert Pattinson," "Carrie Fisher," "Julia Roberts," and "Chris Evans."

Player 1 knows that Player 2 loves Julia Roberts, so he assigns "Julia Roberts" to her, giving the clue: "Brokovich." Within the thirty seconds, Player 2 guesses "Julia Roberts." This is correct, and Player 1 moves on to Player 3. He assigns "Robert Pattinson" to Player 3 with the clue, "Twilight." Player 3 is not able to guess. Player 1 gives a second clue, "Potter." Player 3 correctly guesses "Robert Pattinson," and play continues. Player 1 assigns Player 4 "Carrie Fisher," with the clue "Buns." Player 4 doesn't know. Player 1 gives a second clue, "Space." Player 4 still doesn't know. Player one offers a final clue, "Princess." Player 4 still doesn't know—clearly Player 4 doesn't know *Star Wars* as well as Player 1 had hoped. "Chris Evans" remains for Player 5, and Player 1 offers the clue, "Captain." Player 5 guesses incorrectly, so Player

1 offers a second clue: "Marvel." Player 5 still isn't sure, so Player 1 offers a final clue: "America." Player 5 now correctly guesses "Chris Evans," and the players move onto scoring.

Player 2 guessed correctly after one clue, so Players 1 and 2 both earn 3 points. Player 3 guessed correctly after two clues, so Players 1 and 3 both earn 2 points. Player 4 did not guess, so Players 1 and 4 earn no points. Player 5 guessed after three clues, so Players 1 and 5 earn 1 point. Player 1 earned a total of 6 points out of a possible 12 for his round.

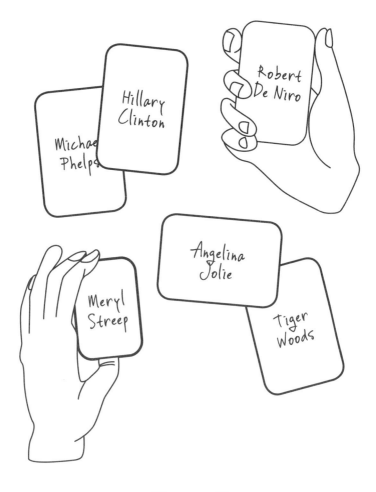

GREED

4+ PLAYERS

> ## GOOD CLUES AND KNOWING WHEN TO QUIT WILL TAKE YOU FAR!

PREPARATION:

Each player writes down approximately twenty common, one-word objects (for example: hammer, television, ear, toaster, camera, computer, iron, bottle, jar, lime, lobster, brick) on separate pieces of paper. No names or proper nouns! These game pieces are all placed together in a hat or other object, preventing anyone from seeing them.

OBJECTIVE:

Players must come up with the best possible clues to earn significant points, and know when to quit when someone else is giving the clues!

GAME TIME:

Player 1 goes first and picks a word out of the hat without revealing it to anyone. She then gives a two-word clue for everyone to guess the word. This is the only clue Player 1 gives! Player 1 cannot use any part of the word in any of the two words of the clue. She can't point to anything or use any hand gestures, and she can't say the word in a foreign language.

Each player then writes down what he thinks the word is, and everyone reveals their answers at once. The players who get it correct then have a choice: they can either "Move on" or "Stop." Those who "Stop" get to keep their points, but they cannot earn any more for that round. Those who move on can earn more points, but they also risk losing all the points they have earned. (Player 1 also earns and loses points as the other players guess, so she must try to give the best possible clues to avoid losing points.)

When the other players have made their choice, Player 1 then picks out another word and prepares a two-word clue for those who elected to move on.

Player 1 must continue until all players have either declared "Stop" or guessed incorrectly and lost their points. When the scores from Player 1's round have been tallied, Player 2 chooses a word and begins giving clues, and so on until all players have had a chance to lead a round.

SCORING:

When a player elects to stop, that player and Player 1 multiply the number of words she guessed correctly by 10, and both that player and Player 1 earn those points for the round.

If a player guesses incorrectly, both that player and Player 1 lose 10 points per word guessed—even if the previous guesses were correct! Players who get the first word wrong lose 10 points and immediately cost Player 1 10 points as well.

EXAMPLE:

If Player 2 guessed six of the words correctly and then declared "Stop," he and Player 1 would both earn 60 points. If Player 3 elected to go for a seventh word and she got it wrong, both Player 3 and Player 1 would lose 70 points each—even though her first six guesses were correct.

Tip: As you see, if a lot of players get too greedy when it is your round to give clues, those players will all lose points, but *you* will lose a lot more! You can set a ten-word maximum per person per round so there is a specific goal for the player giving clues and a limit to the greed for the guessers.

FIGURE OUT THE COMBINATION AND WIN BIG!

PREPARATION:

Each player makes a list of all the players in the game with room next to each player's name to write a number.

Write numbers one through twenty-five on slips of paper and place them in a hat. Each player picks a number out of the hat without showing anyone the number he picked.

Each player must now think of a clue to help the other players decipher his number. Once every player decides on the clue he is going to present, play begins.

OBJECTIVE:

Players must come up with a clue they think most—but not all—players in the game will figure out, and must guess all numbers correctly to unlock the safe and receive important bonus points.

GAME TIME:

Player 1 goes first and gives a clue about his number. All players write down their guesses next to Player 1's name on their sheet without saying them aloud, and then Player 2 gives her clue. Play continues this way until all players have given a clue for their number and everyone has a guess for every player.

Tip: Your code can be anything! Say the number in another language. Come up with a math equation and say it relatively fast so most will get it but at least one person will miss it. Say a famous athlete who wore that number on her jersey. Or perhaps don't use any words at all but scratch your head twenty-four times. Use any method you can think of to get at least one of the players to figure out your number, and to fool at least one player.

Once the final player presents the clue for his number and all guesses are written down, players reveal their actual numbers one at a time and scores are tallied.

SCORING:

Players earn 20 points for each number they guess correctly. Players also earn 10 points for each player who guesses their number correctly. However, if everyone in the game guesses a player's number correctly, that player *loses* 10 points per player in the game. And if no one guesses that player's number correctly, he also loses 10 points per player in the game, and all other players earn 20 points!

EXAMPLE:

Let's say Player 1's number is twenty-four. His clue might be, "The letter 'X.'" Everyone then writes down their guesses next to Player 1's name. Then Player 2 presents her clue to the group. Let's say her number is eleven and her clue is, "The number of players on the field at one time for each team in football." The other players write down their guesses next to Player 2's name, and so on.

Most people in the group may figure out that the letter 'X' is the twenty-fourth letter of the alphabet, and if everyone gets it right, Player 1 loses 10 points per player in the game! If there are a total of 6 players in the game (including Player 1), Player 1 would lose 60 points while everyone else receives 20 points each! Player 2's clue was tougher, though, and if two of the five players guessing could not guess the number, she would earn 30 points (10 for each of the players who guessed correctly).

BONUS POINTS FOR THE CORRECT SAFE COMBINATION:

After all numbers are revealed for every player and points are tallied, bonus points are awarded to every player who guessed every number right and holds the answer to the safe combination! The number of bonus points players receive is equivalent to 10 times the number of players in the game.

For example, in a game of six players, if Player 1 guessed correctly on all five of the other player's numbers, he'd earn 100 points (20 × 5). In addition, Player 1 would earn 60 bonus points (10 × 6 players in the game). Combined with 30 points from the three players who guessed Player 1's number correctly, Player 1's grand total would be 190 points.

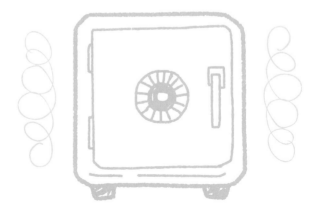

FIND ALL THREE!

3+
PLAYERS

HAVE FUN WITH A STORY ABOUT PEOPLE IN YOUR GROUP

PREPARATION:

Each player has the task of making up a story about two people in the group. Choose any two people. The story should only be one or two sentences and must be no more than thirty words long.

Important: The story cannot be something personal between two people in the group, or a private joke that only a few people in the group know about. It should be a fresh, made-up story.

Once each player has written her story down, each player must choose three of the words from the story and cross out every letter but the first.

OBJECTIVE:

Players must figure out the three words in other stories while selecting the right words to hide in their own stories.

GAME TIME:

Starting with Player 1, players take turns telling their stories. When players read their story to the group, they can only say the first letter of the three words they crossed out. The rest of the group will have to figure out what those words are.

Make the story as silly and fun as desired, but keep in mind the scoring.

SCORING:

Players who are guessing the words earn 20 points if they get all three words right. They earn no points if they get even one word wrong.

The storyteller earns 50 total points if *only one* player gets all three right. However, the storyteller *loses* 50 points if either everyone or no one guesses correctly. She earns 10 total points if more than one person gets it right.

Tip: The challenge of figuring out your three words can't be too easy or too difficult! In either of those cases, you stand to lose a lot of points! For the maximum number of points, you want only one person to figure it out.

EXAMPLE:

Player 1's story might go something like this: "Jack and Linda drove to the s_____ to buy h_____ and hot dogs for the barbecue. While driving there, Jack realized he forgot to wear p____."

The three words missing from Player 1's sentence are "supermarket," "hamburgers," and "pants." If only Player 2 guesses all three words correctly, Player 1 earns 50 points and Player 2 earns 20 points; the other players do not earn any points. If both Players 2 and 3 guess all three words correctly, then they each get 20 points and Player 1 gets only 10. If either everyone or nobody guessed all three words, Player 1 loses 50 points.

FISHING FOR COUPLES

GOING TO THE CHAPEL AND WE'RE GONNA GET MARRIED

PREPARATION:

Each player comes up with ten couples. For this game, a "couple" is any two people or things that are somehow connected. Players can use actual couples like Napoleon and Josephine, Charles and Diana, or Bill and Hillary. Or players can go with Patrick Swayze and Demi Moore from the movie *Ghost*, Robert Redford and Paul Newman from any number of movies they did together, or Michael Jordan and Scottie Pippen, who played together for the Chicago Bulls. Players can even use fictional couples, such as Cinderella and Prince Charming or Han Solo and Princess Leia.

In addition to pairing up well-known people who have some kind of connection, players can go in an entirely different direction and choose pairings like cheddar and swiss, bowl and spoon, chicken noodle and minestrone, spaghetti and linguini, or strawberries and cream. Anything goes. Players write down their couples in a list from one to ten on their paper without letting anyone see. The first half of the couple should be on the left, and will be the clue given to the rest of the group. The second half of the couple will be on the right, and the half the group will try to guess. In other words, for example, write "Salt" on the left and "Pepper" on the right for number one.

OBJECTIVE:

When coming up with couples, to make each one of the ten difficult enough so at least one person doesn't figure it out and easy enough for at least one person to know the answer. When guessing, to figure out as many as possible in the five minutes allotted.

GAME TIME:

Player 1 begins by providing the first half of each of his ten couples as everyone writes them down. Once Player 1 is finished announcing the first half of his ten couples, the rest of the group now has a total of five minutes to guess the second half of each couple. Players should not let anyone see their guesses. After five minutes are up, pens go down! Players pass their answers to the right for that person to score their card (skipping Player 1, who will be busy with his answer key). Once the cards have been passed for scoring, Player 1 reveals the correct answers. One at a time, he reads his correct answers, and the scoring players raise their hands if the player whose paper they have guessed correctly. Player 1 makes a note of how many got each couple right, and the scoring players indicate whether the player they're scoring guessed right or wrong.

SCORING:

The scoring is a major key to the strategy in this game. The guessers receive three points for every correct answer. So, the max score when guessing is 30.

It's a little more complicated for the player coming up with the couples (Player 1 in this case):

First, Player 1 receives 2 points for every correct answer from every player. So, if Player 2 got seven correct, Player 1 would receive 14 points for Player 2's guesses alone. If Player 3 got five correct, Player 1 would receive 10 more points for Player 3's guesses, and so on.

However, it can't be that easy. Otherwise, Player 1 could simply make them all easy and get tons of points while everyone else can get 30 points max by getting them all right! So, here's the twist:

Player 1 doesn't get any points if everyone is correct on a couple. Those players will all get the standard three points for that couple, and Player 1 will get nothing. In addition, if nobody guesses a particular couple, Player 1 also gets no points, and everyone else gets three points!

So, Player 1 must score his own card immediately after the guesses are revealed for each couple and not wait until the end. If four out of the five players got his first couple right, he receives 8 points (4 × 2). However, if everyone or nobody got the couple right, he gets nothing and he lets everyone know they all get three points.

Finally, for every player that guesses only one or two of the ten couples or as many as nine or ten of the couples, Player 1 loses 20 points! So, after all the couples are revealed, players will indicate how many they got right to Player 1. If everyone is between three and eight correct, Player 1 doesn't lose any points. However, for everyone who got one, two, nine, or ten correct, Player 1 loses 20 points each!

Therefore, the ideal scenario for Player 1 has two main components:

1. For every guesser in the game to answer between three and eight correctly
2. Everyone but one person gets each couple right

There are six players in the game. Player 1 gives his ten half-couples, and players all have five minutes to guess. Once the answers are revealed, we learn that for the first two couples, three out of the five guessers got them right. Each of those guessers received three points per correct answer. Player 1 received 12 points (2 × 6 total correct answers for the first two couples). For the next couple, everyone got it right, so they all received three points, but Player 1 received nothing. The next three couples produced a total of nine correct guesses, which gave Player 1 another 18 points (2 × 9). Nobody got the next couple right, so they all received three points and Player 1 got nothing. The final three couples produced a total of eight correct guesses, which gave Player 1 another 16 points (2 × 8). So Player 1 finishes the initial scoring with a total of 46 points. However, we then learn that Player 5 got nine right, and Player 6 only got two right. Therefore, Player 1 loses 40 points (20 each of those two players). Player 1 ends up with a grand total of 6 points for his round.

Player 2 announces the first half of her ten couples and five minutes are put on the clock.

MULTIPLE CHOICES

//

COMBINE STRATEGY WITH TRIVIA

PREPARATION:

Play individually with fewer than eight players. Play teams with eight or more. With an odd number of players above eight, place a third person on one team or have someone play by herself. There are three categories of questions in this game. For maximum point potential, players or teams must come up with three multiple-choice questions with four possible answers, each one belonging to a different category. The three categories are Sports, Arts/Entertainment, and History/Science/Politics. History/Science/Politics is really a grab bag of anything, but that question shouldn't be related to sports or entertainment. Change the category selections if you like, according to the interests of your particular group. Come up with a question in each category and four possible answers for each, and write them all down. If players can't think of a question for one of the categories, they can elect to offer up two or even three questions for one of the categories, but then the point potential will be lower.

OBJECTIVE:

To figure out a way to pose three multiple-choice questions in three different categories where no individual or team will know all the answers, but at least one team will answer each question correctly.

GAME TIME:

Play begins with Player 1 or Team 1 posing their first of three questions. They put thirty seconds on the clock. The other teams now have thirty seconds to privately discuss amongst themselves what they think is the right answer. When the thirty seconds are up, players either hold up A, B, C, or D cards with their guess, or they hold up 1–4 fingers. This is done simultaneously on a count of three. Same goes for the second question from Team 1, and then the third question as well. After each question, Player 1 or Team 1 announces who got it right and records it all on paper. After the guesses are made for the last question and answers are revealed, scoring begins.

SCORING FOR THOSE ANSWERING THE QUESTIONS:

For each question, if your team guesses correctly, your team receives 25 points! If your team gets the right answer for all three questions posed by another team, you receive a bonus 25 points. So, with three questions per player or team, your team can earn a max 100 points (25 × 3, plus 25 bonus points) every time you are guessing. That's the easy part!

SCORING FOR THOSE POSING THE QUESTIONS:

The following very important scoring system will determine the strategy for each team as they determine what kind of questions they want to ask:

When it is your turn to pose your three questions, your team is given 100 points right off the bat only if you have questions in all three categories! If you only used two categories, you begin with 75 points. If you only used one category for all three questions, you begin your round with 50 points.

Here's how you keep or lose those points:

1. If every team gets the answer *right* on one of your questions, your team loses 25 points for that question. In addition, if every team gets the answer *wrong* on one of your questions, you also lose 25 points. So, you can lose 75 points on your turn if one of those scenarios occurs on each question.

2. After your last question is answered by all teams, your team loses 25 points for every team that answered *all* of your questions correctly, and your team loses 25 points for every team that answered all of your questions *incorrectly*!

So, with many other individuals or teams playing the game, you could lose quite a few points on your turn. The ultimate goal is:

- For at least one team to know the answer to every question
- For no question to be answered correctly by every team
- For no team to get them all right or all wrong.

Only when all of these things occur will your team keep all of the points you started with on your turn. That would either be 100, 75, or 50 depending upon how many of the three categories you used.

EXAMPLE:

Team A announces that it has come up with a question for each of the three categories and therefore starts the round with 100 points. The first question is in the sports category.

The question can be anything, from, "Who is the star quarterback for the New England Patriots?" to "What is the width in inches of a paddle ball racket?" As long as Team A knows the correct answer and provides four choices, anything goes!

If two of the three teams guessing get that question right, Team A keeps the 100 points. For the second question in the Entertainment category, let's say all three teams guessing get it wrong. Team A then loses 25 points. Then in the third category, History/Science/Politics, only one team guesses correctly. Team A doesn't lose points because at least one team got it right. Team A still has 75 points. However, it is then revealed that one of the teams got all three questions wrong! Team A then loses another 25 points. The final score for Team A for their round is 50 points. It could have been worse if they had only asked questions in one category and started with 50—they would have then ended up with 0 points on their round.

STRATEGY:

The strategy in coming up with your multiple-choice questions in each category could be for all of the questions to be middle of the road—not too difficult, not too easy. On the other hand, your understanding of every other team's knowledge in certain categories will certainly play into your strategy. You may decide to throw easy questions to a team in each category that you are certain they will know, but fairly sure others won't. It is really all a matter of your understanding of their knowledge on different subjects. In addition, you may determine that you want to use only one or two categories for your questions because your team isn't particularly strong in one of the categories. Let's take Sports, for example. You may not be confident enough in creating good sports questions. Therefore, you would rather forfeit the 25 points at the beginning of your turn, because you will have a better chance of maintaining the rest of your points with more strategic questions in the other one or two categories.

> **Important:** You may not change your questions or multiple-choice options in the middle of your round based on the success of your previous questions. Whichever three questions and four options for each you came up with in the beginning must remain!

NEXT:

Create a whole new set of three questions and play again!

These games are all about speed! Be the first to come up with the answer and you win! Some of these games don't even require paper and pens and are great for passing the time on long road trips.

WITHIN A WORD

3+ PLAYERS

//

BIG WORDS OR SMALL, FIND 'EM FAST. THEY ALL COUNT!

READY, SET, GO!

PREPARATION:

None.

OBJECTIVE:

Find as many words as possible with the letters available. The bigger the word, the more points for that word. However, players who just go for big words may lose to a player with many small words!

GAME TIME:

Player 1 comes up with any six- to ten-letter word. Player 2 then says which letter needs to be removed from the word Player 1 announced. Player 3 says which letter needs to replace that letter. For example, if the original word from Player 1 was "Giraffe," Player 2 may say, "Remove the 'R.'" Player 3 may then say, "Replace the 'R' with the letter 'P.'" The new word is now "Gipaffe." Everyone now has four minutes to come up with as many words as possible that can be made from the letters in "Gipaffe"! Players may only use a letter the same number of times as it appears in the original word. For example, with the word "Gipaffe," you may only have one "I," "A," "G," "P," or "E" in any word you spell, but you can have two "F"s. For example, from the letters in "Gipaffe," you can spell Pig, Fig, Page, Peg, Gap, Gape, Age, Ape, Pea, Gaffe, and so on. No proper nouns! Once the four minutes are up, pens go down! Tally up scores.

SCORING:

Pass your answers to the person to your left. That person will verify that your words are all valid and tally up your score. The number of letters in each word is the number of points you receive for those words. So, if you have four three-letter words and two four-letter words, your total points for the round would be 20! If you have one five-letter word (5), four four-letter words (16), and four three-letter words (12), your total points for that round would be 33.

NEXT:

For the next round, Player 2 comes up with the word, Player 3 removes a letter, and Player 4 replaces that letter.

THAT'S A WISE PURCHASE

3–6 PLAYERS

///

WHAT TO BUY AND WHEN TO BUY

PREPARATION:

Every player comes up with a sentence of a completely made-up and fun "fact" about a person in the game. There can be as many words as you like, but there cannot be any fewer than a total of 25 letters and no more than a total of 40 letters combined with all the words in the sentence.

OBJECTIVE:

Spend as little as possible figuring out each sentence and be the one with the most cash remaining at the end.

GAME TIME:

Player 1 goes first with her sentence, telling the group how many words in her sentence and how many letters in each word so everyone else can draw blanks on their cards or paper. Each player attempting to figure out the puzzle starts out with $100 × the number of letters in the sentence for the total number of points. So, with the maximum of forty letters, each player would start with $4,000. With the minimum of twenty-five letters, each player would start with $2,500. Each player begins round one of this puzzle by handing her card to Player 1 with the specific blanks she wants filled in with letters. Players place an "X" under the blanks they want revealed. It will cost $100 for each letter purchased in the first round. Player 1 fills in the blanks requested with the appropriate letters in her sentence for each player, without showing anyone another player's card. Player 1 also writes the amount of money left at the top of each player's card according to what they purchased. All of the cards are then given back to the respective players at the same time. Once everyone gets their cards back from Player 1, everyone has two minutes to figure out the sentence. Players must not announce the sentence if they figure it out. Simply hand the card to Player 1 for verification. If they are correct, they keep whatever money they have left and note that on a separate score card. Players who have not figured out the sentence after two minutes may buy more letters for $200 each in round two, following the same process. After another two minutes, players can buy more letters for $300 each in round three. That is the final round. Players must complete the phrase in the total six minutes allotted to keep the money they have left after purchases in all three rounds. If not, they will end up with no money for Player 1's sentence.

SCORING:

Players keep track of their earnings for each sentence. Once gameplay is finished, the player with the most money wins!

NEXT:

Players "bank" their earnings on their separate score card and start each round with a clean slate. Player 2 shares the number of words and letters in his sentence and play continues. All players start with $100 × the number of letters in the sentence. Complete a full round with everyone's sentences.

RELATIVES

4+
PLAYERS

//

> **BE THE FASTEST TO FIGURE OUT THE COMMON THEME IN THIS EXCITING TEAM CHALLENGE**

PREPARATION:

First, divide the group into two teams. For each round, all players must come up with a "four-word relative," that is, four words that are all related in some way. (For example, one four-word relative could be "toast," "fries," "onion soup," and "horn." Can you guess the relationship?)

Each of the four words are clues provided one at a time to the other players as they try to find the relation of those words to a specific theme. (In the above case, that theme is "things that are French!") Players should not let any other players, whether on their team or the other team, see their words.

> **Important:** When creating your order of clues, the first and second clues shouldn't give it away easily, but the answer should still be possible to figure out with some creative thinking.

OBJECTIVE:

Players must figure out the theme before the other team. For each round, the faster a player gets it, the more points his team receives.

GAME TIME:

Players from each team take turns providing clues to their four-word relatives while both teams attempt to guess the theme. Player 1 goes first, giving clues one at a time. Players have thirty seconds to guess the theme for each clue. Only one guess, per team, per clue!

Tip: This game is played *Family Feud*-style. The first player on either team to raise his hand after each clue gets one guess. If that person gets the theme wrong in that one guess, the other team has thirty seconds to get together and provide one guess collectively, and so on.

The first team to guess the theme earns points. Then Player 2 gives clues for her four-word relative, and so on.

SCORING:

Teams earn 20 points for guessing the theme after the first clue, 15 points for guessing after the second, 10 points for guessing after the third, and 5 points for guessing after the fourth clue.

EXAMPLES OF RELATIVES:

- King, Queen, Twin, Bunk—Types of beds
- Oklahoma, Mississippi, Sacramento, Concentration—Words with four syllables
- River, Check, Call, Raise—Poker Terms
- Jack, Cliff, Will, Bob—First Names with other meanings

- B12, A1, B1, C7—Gates at the airport
- John, Pete, Keith, Roger—Original members of The Who
- Push, Pull, Lift, Curl—Things you do with weights
- Contract, Jersey, Check, Cast—Things you sign
- Bone, Off, Rex, Cup—Things that go with T-
- Bra, Belt, Clothespin, Sling—Things that hold other things up
- Lions, Tigers, Pistons, Automobiles—Detroit
- Bill Murray, Demi Moore, Dan Aykroyd, Patrick Swayze—"Ghost movie" actors
- Jason, Julia, Michael, Jerry—*Seinfeld* actors
- Alaska, Argentina, Alabama, Aida—Begin and end with the letter "A"
- Raise Arms, Stand Up, Put Arms Down, Sit Down—How to do the wave
- Rabbit, Beetle, Mustang, Taurus—Car models
- "Girl," "Michelle," "Yesterday," "Help"—Beatles songs
- *Glory, Hard Rain, Amistad, Unforgiven*—Morgan Freeman movies
- Chance, Income Tax, Oriental, Park Place—Monopoly
- Emergency, Dark, Bath, Living—Rooms
- Pit, Chair, Rest, Wrestle—Arm stuff
- Balloon, Cookbook, Tattoo, Assassin—Words with two sets of double letters
- Paint, Men, Group, Drums—Blue Man Group
- Cross, Left, Right, Jab—boxing terms
- Pro Golf Match, Broadway Play, Church, Library—Places where you need to be quiet

UNSCRAMBLE ME

3+ PLAYERS

A WORD-SCRAMBLE CHALLENGE WITH A TWIST!

PREPARATION:

Player 1 comes up with a word that is between six and ten letters long and writes it down without letting anyone else see. Player 1 scrambles the word. Player 1 then removes one letter and reads the remaining scrambled letters out loud. The other players write the letters down.

> **Note:** Plural words are not permitted. In other words, "bicycle" is fine, but not "bicycles."

OBJECTIVE:

Players attempt to guess first the missing letter and then the entire word from a list of scrambled letters.

GAME TIME:

Player 1 announces the word's category. The category should be fairly specific, such as "Animal," "US City," "Food," or "Sport." The more specific the category, the faster the game will go.

The first player to figure out the word *does not* say the word out loud! That player only announces the missing letter.

If Player 1 confirms that the missing letter is correct, then the rest of the players add that letter and compete to figure out the word.

> **Important:** The player who said the correct missing letter must be silent and not provide any hint for the rest of the players who are trying to figure out the word.

Play continues as players take turns presenting their scrambled words to the group.

SCORING:

The player who first correctly guesses the missing letter earns 2 points. The rest of the players then compete to be the first to figure out the entire word for 1 point. However, if the player who guessed the missing letter guesses incorrectly, Player 1 must reveal the correct letter, and the other players then have the chance to earn 2 points for guessing the correct word.

> **Important:** When a player guesses the missing letter incorrectly, that player does not get to compete for the two points!

EXAMPLE:

Let's say Player 1 says, "My scrambled word is R-A-N-O-K-A-O, and the category is 'Animal.'" Player 2 figures out that the word is "kangaroo" and the missing letter is "G." Player 2 says, "The missing letter is 'G.'" Player 1 says, "Correct," and Player 2 earns 2 points. The rest of the players now know that the scrambled letters of the complete word are R, A, N, O, K, A, O, and G. If Player 4 is the first to say "kangaroo," Player 4 would earn 1 point.

> **Tip:** You can make this game more challenging by not allowing any writing or by increasing the word length.

BACKWARDS PEOPLE

///

A REVERSE EXPERIENCE!

PREPARATION:

Players take turns coming up with known people (famous people, or people everyone in the game knows). Pronounce the name backwards, first name then last!

Tip: It is much easier if you write the first and last name down backwards first so you can look at it before you pronounce it.

GAME TIME:

Players guessing cannot write down what they hear. (That's way too easy!) The first player to guess the name earns 1 point.

EXAMPLES:

- NHOJ ATLOVART
- YTTEB SIVAD
- ODRANOEL OIRPACID
- AIRAM AVOPARAHS

Answers: John Travolta, Betty Davis, Leonardo DiCaprio, Maria Sharapova

I SEE YOU!

LOOK CAREFULLY—THE
WORD WILL REVEAL ITSELF
EVENTUALLY!

PREPARATION:

Each player thinks of a seven- to ten-letter word. Without showing anyone, players write the word down with spaces in between the letters in order to place ten other random letters in the word.

A word such as "computer" would look something like this:

CLKAOMURPUSYOTIEAR

(The letters of the word "computer" are only underlined for this example to show you where it is in the long line of letters.)

OBJECTIVE:

Players attempt to be the first to find the hidden word!

GAME TIME:

Player 1 goes first and reads her long list of letters from left to right so everyone can write them down. Players begin to try to find the word and guess what it is. Every twenty seconds, Player 1 tells the other players to cross out a specific letter (one of the extra letters). Using the above example, she may say things like, "Cross out the 'K,'" or, "Cross out the first 'A,'" or, "Cross out the last 'O.'" The first person to guess the word wins the round and earns points.

Player 2 then reads his list of letters, and so on.

SCORING:

The sooner a player guesses the word, the more points she earns. If a player guesses the word before Player 1 crosses off the first letter, she earns 100 points. For every letter Player 1 crosses off, players earn 10 fewer points (subtracting from 100). (For example, if you guess the word after Player 1 crosses off four letters, you earn 60 points.) The first player to 500 points wins!

MISSING VOWELS

3+ PLAYERS

TWWRNGSDNTMKRGHT

PREPARATION:

Every player comes up with a common or well-known phrase, proverb, sentence, or even a line or quote from a song which contains at least ten consonants. Write the phrase down on a piece of paper in one long line without any spaces in between the words, leaving out the letters A, E, I, O, and U. Don't let anyone see the phrase.

OBJECTIVE:

As the letters are revealed, figure out the phrase before anyone else for maximum points.

GAME TIME:

Player 1 goes first with his phrase by first letting everyone know how many total letters he will be providing so everyone makes enough room on their paper. Player 1 slowly reveals letters by spelling the phrase backwards, from last letter to first, while everyone writes them down. For example, the phrase "When the going gets tough, the tough get going" would look like this on his paper: WHNTHGNGGTSTGHTHTGHGT-GNG. Player 1 would begin with the last G and everyone would write it on the right side of their own paper, and then when Player 1 provides another letter, they place that letter to the left of the previous letter. This way, when all letters are provided, players would be able to read the entire phrase from left to right. However, it may not take that long for a player to figure it out. For some of these phrases, a player might see it after the first few letters if he figures out the last word and wants to take a guess. For others, it may take staring at the entire phrase for a little while to figure it out. Once Player 1 finishes announcing all of the letters, a two-minute timer begins. If nobody has guessed after two minutes, then Player 1 will start to reveal the missing vowels from right to left every five seconds as players begin to guess.

SCORING:

The second someone thinks they have it figured out, that person says, "Got it!" Do not shout out the answer! The player writes his guess down under the string of letters and then turns his paper over, writes a big number 1 on the back, and keeps that side face-up so nobody can see his guess. This means he was the first to take a guess and potentially figure it out. The next person to figure it out says, "Got it!" and follows the same process as the first player who guessed, but this player writes a big number 2 on the back of his paper. The guesses should be face-down for nobody to see; the numbers are face-up. The third person to guess does the same. After that, nobody else can guess. All three guesses are then revealed and points are tallied. The first person who guessed reveals his answer first. If he was correct, he receives 20 points. If he was wrong, he gets nothing. The second person who guesses correctly receives 10 points and the third person receives 5 points. If the first guesser was wrong, the second guesser would get 20 points if he was right and the third would get 10. If both the first and second guessers were wrong, they would get nothing and the third guesser would get 20 if he was right.

NEXT:

For the next round, Player 2 shares her long string of consonants in her phrase.

PICK A CARD

3–8
PLAYERS

**INDEX CARDS
RECOMMENDED**

//

HOW MUCH OF A RISK ARE YOU WILLING TO TAKE?

PREPARATION:

Player 1 comes up with a word that is at least six letters long within a specific category of his choice. The category will be shared with the group. Categories could be anything, such as "Sports," "Animals," "Vegetables," "Occupations," "Countries," and so on. For example, if your category is "Countries," you may decide on "Argentina." Now you must write out the word "Argentina" on nine separate index cards, with each of the nine letters in "Argentina" on a separate card. In addition, if you have a word where the same letter is used multiple times, you must indicate that next to those letters. For example, with Argentina, there are two "A"s and two "N"s. So, place a one next to one of the A letters and a two next to the other A letter. Same for the N letters. Therefore, if someone picks one of them from the pile, that person will see either A1, A2, N1, or N2 and will know that this letter is in the word more than once. Player 1 doesn't let anyone see her letters, mixes them up, and places them all in a pile in front of her, face-down. While Player 1 is doing this, the other players are thinking of the word and category they will use on their turn so they have it ready to go and only have to write it on the index cards on their turn. The number of index cards used is equivalent to the number of letters in the chosen word. However, in order to not waste cards, Player 2 will cross out the letters on the cards Player 1 used and write his word on as many of those cards as necessary, adding new cards if his word is longer.

OBJECTIVE:

To figure out the word in as few clues as possible for maximum points.

GAME TIME:

Player 1 goes first. She announces her category and places her mixed-up cards in a hat or face-down on the table so every other player can pick a random card, look at it, and put it back. If there are more players guessing than letters in the word, the player(s) left without a card will wait for others to put their cards back in the hat or on the table so they can pick a card as well for round one. When picking up a card, don't let anyone see it. Players may then make a note on a separate piece of paper as to what they picked. Once all letters are back in the pile, players will have the option of guessing the word for 10 points or getting another clue. If a player wants to guess the word, he writes it on a separate piece of paper and places it face-down in front of him, with the number ten on the part that is face-up. This player cannot guess again or get any other clues. He will have to wait until all players have made a guess and Player 1 reveals the word. Next, players will pick again from the pile. The pile should always be mixed again if on the table in plain sight so the pick is completely random. Again, if a player wants to guess after the second clue, she will write her guess on a piece of paper and place it face-down in front of her, this time with the number nine on the face-up part. For each clue, drop the number by one when making a guess. For example, after four clues, the number you write on the paper with your guess is seven. After six clues, the number is five. There is a max of ten clues. After that, players can guess and place a number one on their paper, or they can decline to guess. The strategy is all about the scoring.

It is all about when you decide to take a guess. If you take a guess after the first clue and have a 10 on your paper, you risk losing 10 points if you are wrong. If you are right, however, you will earn 10 points, plus a bonus 5 points for guessing after one clue. If you decide to guess after the second clue, you will either earn or lose 9 points, depending upon whether you end up being right or wrong. No bonus points. The same goes for every other guess after more clues. You either get the points written on the top of your paper or lose them. A guess after ten clues means you will either get a point or lose a point. However, if you decide not to guess after the final clue, you will end the round with 0 points.

> **Reminder:** Remember, for each clue you simply pick up the card, look at the letter and place it back without letting anyone see. You can then write on your separate piece of paper the letter you picked.

For the next round, Player 2 quickly writes his word on the separate index cards, places them in a hat or mixed face-down on the table, and gives everyone his category.

TWINS

IT'S A RACE TO FIND THE PAIR!

PREPARATION:

Each player thinks of two words that have something in common, such as "baseball" and "basketball," "trumpet" and "trombone," "airport" and "terminal," and so on. No plurals allowed! Players draw blanks in a line representing the number of letters in the two words if they were placed next to each other. (For example, with "baseball" and "basketball," the total number of letters in both words combined is eighteen: "baseballbasketball.")

OBJECTIVE:

Players attempt to be the first to find the pair.

GAME TIME:

Using the example of baseball and basketball, Player 1 goes first and tells the other players to draw eighteen blanks. Player 1 then tells everyone to place specific letters one at a time over specific blanks. Every fifteen seconds, he provides one letter until someone shouts out what she thinks the two words are. However, Player 1 must provide the letter clues in the following sequence:

1. First letter of the first word
2. Last letter of the second word
3. Second letter of the first word
4. Second-to-last letter of the second word
5. Third letter of the first word
6. And so on

After seven letters are placed with the example of "base-ballbasketball," the line should look like this:

base_ _ _ _ _ _ _ _ _ _all

Play continues as players take turns coming up with "twin" words.

The first player to figure out the two words and shout out the correct answer earns 5 points for that round. However, if players guess incorrectly, they are out of the round (only one guess per player per round). In addition, each time a player shouts out a wrong guess, the prize for the correct answer increases by 5 points for the rest of the players competing. So, if two players shout out the wrong answer, the prize is now 15 points to the player who shouts out the right answer. The first player to earn 100 points wins!

READY, SET, GO!

ADD 'EM UP!

3+ PLAYERS

> ## WORD MATH—IT'S MORE FUN THAN IT SOUNDS.

PREPARATION:

Draw a chart on a piece of paper with all of the letters of the alphabet corresponding to a number from 1 to 26 (A = 1, B = 2, C = 3, and so on to Z = 26), and place it on the table so all players can see it.

OBJECTIVE:

Players attempt to come up with more words than everyone else in each round!

GAME TIME:

Player 1 goes first and picks whether the challenge will be three-, four- or five-letter words. Player 2 then picks one letter which must be used as the first letter of each word. Player 3 then decides on a ten-point range which must be achieved.

> **Note:** To come up with an appropriate ten-point range: Three-letter words should be within 10–60 points. Four-letter words should be within 20–75 points. Five-letter words should be within 30–90 points.

Player 1 sets a five-minute timer and, all at once, each player must try to come up with as many words as possible that meet the chosen criteria (length, starting letter, and point range). When time is up, players tally their points, and the next round begins with Player 2 selecting the number of letters in the words, Player 3 choosing a letter that must be used, and Player 4 selecting a specific 10-point range. The round after that, Player 3 selects the number of letters in the word, Player 4 chooses a letter that must be used, and so on.

Regardless of the length of each word, players earn one point per word that meets all three criteria. The number of correct words players come up with is the number of points they receive for that round.

EXAMPLE:

Let's say Player 1 picks five-letter words, Player 2 says the letter "C" must be the first letter of each word, and Player 3 says the points should be between 41 and 50. (You can choose any 10-point range, but we advise that you stay within the guidelines listed above according to the total number of letters being used.) Once the timer starts, every player tries to come up with as many five-letter words as possible that begin with the letter "C" and will be worth between 41 and 50 points. The word "crush" has a total of 69 points, so it would not make the list: C = 3, R = 18, U = 21, S = 19, and H = 8. The word "clamp," however, has a total of 45 points (C = 3, L = 12, A = 1, M = 13, and P = 16), so the player would receive a point for that word.

THAT'S ENTERTAINMENT

3+
PLAYERS

///

A SPEEDY CHALLENGE PERFECT FOR FANS OF POP CULTURE

PREPARATION:

Player 1 thinks of an actor and a movie and gives a three-letter clue. The first two are the first letters of the actor's first and last names; the third letter is the first letter of the title of a movie he or she starred in.

> **Tip:** Be sure to leave articles (the, a, an) out of the movie titles.

> **Note:** This game can be played with other categories as well: singer and band, author and book, singer and song, and so on. This example will use actors and movies, but the possibilities are endless!

OBJECTIVE:

Players attempt to be the first to guess the actor and movie based on the three letters given.

Players have sixty seconds to guess the actor and movie based solely on the three letters. If no one can guess it after sixty seconds, players take turns asking for additional clues, such as, "Give us the second letter of the actor's first name," or, "Give us the second letter of the movie title." The first player to guess the actor and the movie wins the round and receives points.

Player 2 now thinks of an actor and a movie, gives a three-letter clue, and so on.

SCORING:

If a player guesses correctly in the first sixty seconds, she earns 10 points. After each additional clue, subtract 2 points from 10. (In other words, if someone guesses the actor and movie correctly after one clue, that player earns 8 points; after two clues, 6 points; three clues, 4 points; four clues, 2 points.) Players can earn only 1 point after more than four clues have been given. The first player to earn 50 points wins!

EXAMPLES:

- APS (Al Pacino, *Scarface*)
- TCM (Tom Cruise, *Mission Impossible*)
- WFA (Will Ferrell, *Anchorman*)

FOUND IT

//

JUST FIND IT ALREADY!

PREPARATION:

Each player creates his own puzzle for the rest of the group to figure out! Draw a grid of four rows across and four down containing sixteen boxes. Spell any word between seven and twelve letters in the grid by placing one letter from the word in each box. All letters in the word have to be touching either vertically, horizontally, or diagonally in order. So, with the word "Simplify", the S must be touching the I, which must be touching the M, which must be touching the P, and so on. Fill in the remaining empty boxes with other random letters. Players turn over their grid and wait until it's their turn to offer up a puzzle.

OBJECTIVE:

Be the first to find the word in each grid!

GAME TIME:

Player 1 goes first with his puzzle. Everyone else draws a blank grid of sixteen boxes to fill in with Player 1's letters. Player 1 tells everyone where to put each letter in his grid from left to right, starting with the first row at the top. Once

everyone fills in the grid with the letters Player 1 provided, Player 1 then tells the players how many total letters are in his word, along with the starting letter of his word.

Tip: Some of the random letters in your grid can be the same as the first letter of your word to throw people off.

The first person to figure out the word and shout it out wins! If more than two minutes go by without a guess, every thirty seconds Player 1 tells the players to cross off a specific letter in the grid that isn't in the word. Do this until only the letters in the word remain. If nobody figures it out after that, offer up the next letter in the word and then the next every thirty seconds until someone shouts it out.

SCORING:

One point for every grid you figure out!

NEXT:

Player 2 provides the letters in her grid to the group for everyone to figure out.

PHONETICALLY SPEAKING

EVERYONE WINS THIS SPELLING BEE

PREPARATION:

Each player must come up with a word that can be spelled differently phonetically. For example, the word "Education" can be spelled a few different ways by simply sounding it out and using letters that corresponded to the sounds. How about "Edgeookayshun"? Or "Ejewkaishun"? Or "Ejookation"? There are obviously several possibilities for this word. The word "Elephant" could possibly be spelled "Elifint" or "Elefent." Both are pretty close when sounding them out. There is no right answer here. It really doesn't matter how it's spelled, as long as the phonetic spelling can be justified and people can understand the word. Once players have a good phonetic word, they write it on a paper without anyone seeing and turn it over face-down in front of them.

OBJECTIVE:

Be the first to find the phonetically spelled word!

Player 1 begins the game with her word. She starts by giving everyone the number of letters in her word. Each player then places blanks on his paper with numbers from one to the number of letters in the word from left to right underneath each blank. This game is played Hangman-style. One at a time, players take turns asking if a specific letter is in the word and Player 1 says where it goes if the letter is in the word. First person to guess the original word ("Education," in this case) wins!

If you raise your hand first and guess the word by pronouncing it, you get 5 points. If there is still at least one letter left blank when you guess it and you can then spell it the way Player 1 spelled it, you get a bonus 2 points. If the first player guesses the word correctly but not the spelling, he only earns 5 points and the other players have the opportunity to guess the spelling for 2 points. The other players then write their guesses down and reveal them to Player 1. Every player that gets it right gets the 2 points. If a player guesses the word and is wrong, he cannot guess again and is out of the round! Players continue to guess the word until someone gets it right for 5 points, and then spells it correctly for the 2 bonus points.

Player 2 provides the number of letters in her word and everyone else takes a shot.

THIRD-BASE COACH

READY, SET, GO!

IT'S ALL ABOUT THE SIGNALS AND TRYING TO CRACK THE CODE!

PREPARATION:

Break up the group into two teams. One player in each round won't be on a team. That player (Player 1, for example) will come up with the category and word and will be giving signs to everyone else. Each team must come up with a sign for Player 1 to use when she wants to indicate that a letter the team is asking about is in her word. Teams should come up with a sign, such as "Touch nose twice," or, "Pat self on the butt," or, "Act like a chicken," or, "Do a cartwheel." Anything goes! Teams won't reveal their team sign to anyone except Player 1. While teams are coming up with a sign, Player 1 is determining a word she will be playing within a specific category. Categories could be anything, such as "Sports," "Animals," "Vegetables," "Occupations," "Countries," and so on.

OBJECTIVE:

Figure out the word before the other team by using clues from the third base coach, while trying to also crack the other

team's code and employing a guessing strategy which would potentially throw them off their trail.

Player 1 goes first and reveals her category. Let's say her category is "Sports" and her word is "Wrestling." She says her category out loud to both teams and keeps her word to herself. (The word can be written down on a piece of paper face-down in front of her so nobody sees it, or she simply keeps it to herself if there are no pens and paper in the game.) Each team then either whispers their sign to Player 1 or gives Player 1 a piece of paper with their sign on it. When Player 1 performs the sign, that is the indicator that the letter asked about is in the word. Next, the team chosen to go first (Team A) asks Player 1 about two different letters that may be in the word. Team A may say, "We want to know about the letters 'O' and 'R.'" Then Player 1 will begin by saying, "These are the signs for the letter 'O:'" and then she proceeds to give a whole bunch of signs like a third base coach, which will either incorporate the sign provided by that team or not based on whether or not the letter "O" is actually in the word. For the word "Wrestling," she will make sure not to give that team their sign, since there is no "O" in "Wrestling." However, after she is finished with those signs, she will then announce the next series of signs for the letter "R." For the word "Wrestling," this time she will have to include that team's sign so that they are now aware her word includes an "R." Team A will now have thirty seconds to guess the word if they wish to take a guess. Taking a guess could give a hint as to the answers they just received about their two letters, or they can make a false guess to throw the other team off their trail. It's their decision either way. Next, Team B gets to ask about two letters of their own and Player 1 will make sure she knows their sign and will begin the signing process again for

READY, SET, GO!

them. Player 1 must make sure to offer a series of signs each time and to carefully disguise them so it will make it difficult for each team to figure out the other team's code.

Finally, after four rounds each of providing signs for eight letters to each team, if no team has come up with the answer, there is a lightning round. For the lightning round, each team gets to ask about a letter and Player 1 must say whether the letter is in the word out loud to the entire group. In the lighting round, each team can only take one guess after each answer is provided, but there is no order to guessing! First team to shout it out wins! If nobody knows, the next team asks for a letter, and so on until the answer is shouted by a team.

Each player on the team that figures it out earns 1 point. The player coming up with the word doesn't score.

New teams are organized and Player 2 is the third base coach with his word.

READY, SET, GO!

DON'T TELL FRANK
HE'S GOING BALD

HANGMAN WITH PERSONALITY

PREPARATION:

Each player puts together a five- to seven-word sentence about someone else in the game without revealing the sentence to the other players.

The sentence can be about anyone and doesn't have to be a true statement.

OBJECTIVE:

Players attempt to be the first to guess the sentence.

GAME TIME:

Player 1 begins by telling the other players how many words are in his sentence and how many letters are in each word. On their own sheets of paper, the other players draw blanks representing the letters in each word of the sentence. Then everyone places numbers under each blank from left to right, starting with 1 as the first letter of the first word, 2 as the second letter of the first word, and so on. (Spaces and punctuation don't count.) If there are only three letters in the first word, then the number 4 would be the first letter of the second word, and so on.

The phrase "Don't tell Frank he's going bald" would look like this:

_ _ _ ' _ / _ _ _ _ / _ _ _ _ _ / _ _ ' _ / _ _ _ _ _ / _ _ _ _
1 2 3 4 5 6 7 8 9 10 11 12 13 14 15 16 17 18 19 20 21 22 23 24 25

Players take turns asking Player 1 to fill in a specific letter. If Player 2 begins by selecting "N," Player 1 would then tell everyone where the letter "N" goes. In the example, Player 1 would say, "'N' goes above the numbers 3, 12, and 20." If Player 3 then asks for the letter "A," Player 1 would then say, "'A' goes in slots 11 and 23."

Players take turns asking for a letter until one player shouts out the correct sentence and wins the round. If a player shouts out the wrong sentence, that player is out of the round and has no more guesses.

Player 2 goes next, sharing the number of words in her sentence and the number of letters in each word, and so on.

SCORING:

A player wins one point for every phrase he guesses correctly. The person with the most correct guesses after everyone takes a turn with his phrase, wins.

CLUE SCRAMBLER

3+
PLAYERS

READY, SET, GO!

PREPARATION:

Each player comes up with one of two things:

1. A fun, two- to five-word "category clue" that can
   be used to describe a specific group of people
2. A two- to five-word "personal description clue"
   that is used to describe one specific person.

A "category clue" to describe a specific group of people would be something like "Late-Night Talk Show Host,"
"Western European Leader," "Female Reality TV Star,"
"Popular Nightly Newscaster," "Famous Tech Billionaire,"
"Famous Hockey Player," or "Action Movie Star." These are
all clues that describe more than one person, but are specific
enough that when people try to guess a person, it shouldn't
take too long to figure out.

On the other hand, a two- to five-word "personal descrip-
tion clue" would be something like, "Female Star of *Pretty
Woman*," "Current American President," or "Rolling Stones
Lead Singer." These all describe one specific person.

Either way, players must think of a specific person they
want people to figure out. Once they have that person, they

must then decide on the type of clue they want to give—either a category clue or a personal description clue.

As soon as players have their person and clue, they scramble the letters of each word in their clue and write the clue down in the right word order. Then they write the name of the person under the scrambled words and turn the paper over.

OBJECTIVE:

To be the first to guess the name of the person the player is thinking of in each round.

GAME TIME:

Player 1 goes first and tells everyone how many words are in his clue, and then he says out loud the letters of each word in the scrambled order so everyone can write them down. He doesn't tell anyone if this is a category clue or a personal description clue.

For example, let's say Player 1 decided he wants people to guess Wayne Gretzky and he chose the category clue "Famous Hockey Player." He gave everyone his scrambled clue, which looked like this: MOFUSA KEYOHC LYREPA.

Players are now in a race to unscramble the words and figure out the clue. Once a player figures it out, he doesn't tell anyone what the clue is! He simply starts shouting out answers until Player 1 confirms the right answer. If it is a "personal description clue" such as "*Pretty Woman* Lead Actress" and the player knows it is Julia Roberts, the game will be over if he is the first to get the clue. However, in the case of "Famous Hockey Player," there are several options. For those who know the game of hockey, Wayne Gretzky would be as good a guess as it gets, but he certainly isn't the only famous hockey player.

Tip: The trick with the "category clues" is that once you start guessing names, other players can now join in

SCORING:

1 point per player who figures out the name for each round.

NEXT:

Every player takes a turn trying to get people to figure out his scrambled clues and name.

WHAT'S MY FOUR-LETTER WORD?

3+
PLAYERS

//

**BE THE FASTEST TO GUESS THE
FOUR-LETTER WORD WITHOUT
ANY WRITING!**

PREPARATION:

Players think of a four-letter word and then come up with four three-letter words that are clues to figuring out the four-letter word. Each of the four three-letter words must contain a letter that is in the four-letter word. No writing allowed!

> **Note:** The three-letter words don't have to have anything to do with the four-letter word. The only requirement is that each of them contain one of the letters found in the four-letter word.

OBJECTIVE:

Players take turns giving clues for their four-letter words and try to be the first to guess the other players' words.

Player 1 gives the three-letter words in order, with the first letter of the four-letter word somewhere in the first clue, the second letter of the four-letter word somewhere in the second clue, and so on. The first player to guess the four-letter word wins the round and earns 1 point.

Play continues as Player 2 gives clues for her four-letter word, and so on.

SCORING (6+ PLAYERS):

With six or more players, players earn 1 point for guessing a four-letter word correctly, and the first player to earn 5 points wins.

SCORING (FEWER THAN 6 PLAYERS):

With three to five players, the first player to earn 3 points wins. However, players who aren't the first person to guess the word lose 1 point each time!

For example, if Player 4 guesses the first word from Player 1, she gets 1 point. If she guesses the next one from Player 2, she gets another point for a total of 2. She can now win the game with three points if she is the first to guess the next one from Player 3. However, if Player 5 guesses the next one from Player 3, then Player 5 gets 1 point and Player 4 loses a point, going back to 1. If Player 2 guesses the next one, then both Player 4 and Player 5 go back to 0. (Players never go into negative points, though; they just stay at zero.)

Important: When it is your turn to come up with a four-letter word and give clues, your current points freeze until after your turn.

- Four-Letter Word: prom; Clues: pig, art, old, arm
- Four-Letter Word: flag; Clues: off, lot, bar, rug
- Four-Letter Word: jump; Clues: jog, mud, ham, tap

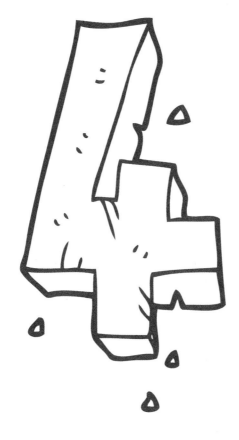

H ere are nine fun games to test your memory. How well can you remember what you have seen or heard? What kind of memory techniques can you use to get a leg up on your competition? Even those who typically struggle with memorization can have a great time playing these games.

CIRCLE OF EMOTIONS

4+ PLAYERS

//

TRY TO REMEMBER

HAVING TONS OF FUN REMEMBERING WHO DID WHAT

PREPARATION:

Each player writes five different emotions or actions on separate pieces of paper and places them in the middle of the table. Any emotions that can be acted out will do, such as anger, fear, sadness, joy, amazement, surprise, shame, tenderness, excitement, and so on. Or you can get really creative and submit specific actions, such as, "Afraid of a bee stinging you" or "Walking into a glass door" or "Someone licking your face." Mix all of the emotions face-down in the middle of the table. Next, players take a separate piece of paper and write everyone's name in the left-hand column, with theirs at the top. Leave enough room to the right of everyone's name to list emotions.

OBJECTIVE:

To remember who exhibited each emotion.

GAME TIME:

With four players, each player picks out four random emotions from the pile. With five to seven players, each player picks out three emotions from the pile. With eight to eleven players, each player picks out two emotions. With twelve or more, each player picks out one emotion. Players can adjust these numbers according to the strengths or weaknesses of the group when it comes to memory.

If a player can't read an emotion, throw it out and pick a new one from the master pile. (You can't just throw one out because you don't like it! Only if you can't read it!) Next, players write their emotions on their guessing card next to their name at the top, in the order in which they would like to act them out. Once players have written their order, pens go down and stay down! One at a time, beginning with Player 1, everyone has five seconds to act out their first emotion— no words allowed!. Players go around the table, watching everyone act out their first emotion and trying to remember what they see as best as they can. Then Player 1 acts out her second emotion, and then Player 2, and so on, until everyone is done acting out all of their emotions. Next, all of the emotions are discarded into a new pile. Don't mix them with the emotions that weren't picked. One player is selected to pick them up, mix them up face-down and read them out loud one at a time. Everyone can now pick up their pens. When an emotion is read, players write it down next to the player on the sheet that they believe acted out that emotion. They must write it legibly, since someone else will be scoring the card. Players shouldn't ever give away who they think it is! Once all emotions are read, players may move around emotions and come to a final decision of who acted out each one. Make sure the list is clear and pass it to the player to the right.

SCORING:

Players go around the room announcing what emotions they acted out as everyone scores the cards in front of them. Players earn 1 point for every emotion they get right. In addition, the player who acted out the emotions gets a point for every player who guessed each emotion correctly.

So, let's say there are six total players in the game, and each player acted out three emotions. That means in addition to getting points for guessing, each player can earn an additional 15 points maximum if the other five players remembered all of her emotions correctly. Therefore, when emoting, you want to make it memorable and easy for people to understand to earn maximum points!

After each player announces the emotions she acted out, the other players must tell her how many additional points she received from those who got it right.

Note: There may be duplicate emotions. For example, two people may have submitted "sad" to the pile and three people may have submitted "happy" to the pile. Therefore, you would have several people acting out those same emotions. However, there may be very different types of sadness, happiness, and so on performed, so you may end up changing your guesses at the end once all of the emotions are read.

NEXT:

If you wish to play again, have everyone submit a whole new set of five emotions to a new pile if there aren't enough left to play a second round. Don't use the same emotions twice.

ALPHABET CITY

4+
PLAYERS

**LONG WORDS WILL SCORE BIG,
BUT REMEMBERING THEM ALL
IS THE TRUE ADVANTAGE**

PREPARATION:

Every player chooses a letter and announces it. Players can't choose the same letter as someone else, so make sure everyone announces what letter they are going with. Write the letter on the back of an index card. On the front, come up with words that begin with that letter and list them legibly in all caps. No made-up words or technical words; they should be words everyone in the group has heard before.

The number of words players must list is equal to the number of players in the game (minus themselves) times three. So, with seven total players in the game, players must list eighteen words (6 × 3) that begin with the chosen letter. Next to each word, players write the number of letters in the word. This is also the number of points a player will receive for remembering that word.

Important: The total number of letters combined with all of your words must be at least six times the number of words you are listing. So, with seven players in the

TRY TO REMEMBER

game and eighteen words on your card, the total number of letters in all words combined must be at least 108 (18 × 6). In addition, the different words on your list must be at least four different lengths. In other words, all of your words can't be six letters. With eighteen words, you can have five four-letter words (20 points), five six-letter words (30 points), four eight-letter words (32 points) and four ten-letter words (40 points) if you like. (Total points = 122.) Or some other mix like that.

Place the card with all the words and numbers face-down.

To remember as many words as possible on each turn to have the best chance of scoring. Score the most overall points to win!

GAME TIME AND SCORING:

Pens go down and stay down. Player 1 begins with his card and sets a thirty-second timer. Every player now has thirty seconds to study the words on Player 1's card, taking note of the number next to it. Player 1 times everyone for thirty seconds, saying "Pass" when it is time for the player to pass the card to his right. Play officially begins for the round when the last player has studied the card for thirty seconds.

Player 2 goes first and gets to choose how many points she wants to go for with this letter. She says out loud which point total she wants to go for and then says the word out loud. She has fifteen seconds to do this—no more! If she chooses a twelve-point word and Player 1 confirms she got it right, Player 2 will get twelve points. Player 1 writes her name down next to that word and number and circles it all; the word is now out of play. If Player 2 gets it wrong, she doesn't lose any points—she just won't be able to score until her turn comes around again. Player 3 then decides how many points he wants to go for and says a word he remembers from the list with that many letters. Play continues with Player 4 and so on, until all of the other players have had a chance to score from Player 1's card. Players go three times around the table, since there are always three times the number of words as there are players guessing. This way, every player has the chance to score three times on another player's card.

Then Player 2 announces her letter and begins the thirty-second timer for each player to study her card, and play begins again with Player 3 having the first turn.

STRATEGY:

When coming up with your list of words, if you go well over the minimum total points needed, then you risk giving out more points to your opponents on your turn than you will have the chance to earn on everyone else's turn. On the other hand, many bigger words may be more difficult to remember, so that could be a factor in your word choice as well. If you're offering a lot of points but nobody can remember your big words, you may not end up giving out many points at all. Just keep in mind that your words should all be mainstream words—no technical words or words only known to a select few in your group.

Obviously, Player 2 has the advantage with Player 1's card by going first on her turn to earn points and select the biggest word. However, Player 2 was also the first person to study Player 1's card, so the words are less fresh in her memory. Play rotates around the room so each player begins and ends studying cards and taking turns in every possible position. With a big group (more than six players), you can have everyone make two of the same card so you can pass around your two cards in two different directions. This will make the studying time go a lot faster for everyone.

LAST NIGHT

4+ PLAYERS

///

> ## REMEMBERING EVERYONE'S BASKETBALL TEAM

PREPARATION:

Every player must come up with five famous people and write each of them on separate pieces of paper or index cards face-down on the table. Someone mixes them all up together without looking at any of them. Next, players write the name of every player in the game on another paper (including their own at the top) and make sure there is enough room to write in five famous people to the right of everyone's name.

OBJECTIVE:

To remember as many of the players on everyone's team as possible for the maximum points.

GAME TIME:

Pens go down! Make sure the pile of famous people is mixed and in a pile face-down. Players are now ready to form their starting basketball teams of five players each. Player 1 begins by picking up the pile and saying something like, "Last night, I went to dinner with . . ." and then she turns over the first card and announces who came to dinner with her. Let's say it was Marlon Brando. She will have said, "Last night, I went to dinner with Marlon Brando." Player 1 then places the Marlon Brando card face-down in front of her and passes the deck to Player 2. Player 2 will then say something like, "Last night I ate chocolate cookies with . . ." and he turns the next card over, saying who it is. The bottom line is that each player gets to say whatever she likes about what exactly she did last night, and then reveals who participated in the activity with her. Players want to say something memorable, because the more people who remember the players on their team, the more bonus points they will get. Player 2 places his famous person face-down in front of him and then hands the deck to Player 3. Keep the game moving. Players should be ready to say what it is they did last night after the previous person goes. Play goes around five times until everyone has announced the five people who are on their teams. The object is for a player to remember who is on everyone's team as best as possible, including their own! Once the last person goes, players can pick their pens back up and start filling in the famous people they remember everyone announcing next to each player's name on the paper, including the members of their own team. Players may not pick up any of the cards, including their own. Everyone has only five minutes on the clock to remember as many names as she can! Players may only list five people next to each player's name—no more. Each player passes her answers to the player to her right. That player will score the card.

SCORING:

Player 1 goes first: she picks up her five cards and starts reading off the members of her team. Circle the name of everyone on the sheet in front of you that the player you're scoring got right. Each player gets 1 point per player that she remembered on Player 1's team. Then Player 1 asks each player how many the player they are scoring got right. That is how many bonus points Player 1 gets. So, if Player 3 remembered four people on Player 1's team, Player 1 would get 4 bonus points. If Player 4 remembered three people on Player 1's team, Player 1 would get 3 more bonus points, and so on. If Player 1 remembered all of her own players, she gets 5 points but no bonus points from herself. Player 1 totals up how many players on her team were remembered by all of the other players in the game for her bonus points. So, it could look like this:

- Player 2 = 3
- Player 3 = 4
- Player 4 = 3
- Player 5 = 1
- Player 6 = 1
- Total bonus points for Player 1 = 12
- Total points tallied for Player 1 = 17 (12 bonus points plus 5 for remembering all of her own)

Next, Player 2 reveals the members of his team, and now he gets bonus points based on how memorable his team was for everyone in the game. Total up all of your points after the last person reveals his team to determine the winner.

4+ PLAYERS

IT'S ALL IN THE DETAILS

PREPARATION:

Each player in the game takes a piece of paper or large index card and writes numbers on the left side from one to ten. Then they make four columns for each of the ten rows.

Players must make up ten very memorable stories about specific people they met somewhere at some time. All of these stories are completely made-up.

Each story must have four important details:

1. Who is the person?
2. Where did you meet?
3. What specific activity did you do with that person?
4. What specific food did you eat together?

For example, for your first story, you can say, "I met John Lennon at a Beatles concert. We played guitar and we ate fish and chips." That story includes the four details necessary for each story. Who? John Lennon. Where? Beatles concert. What did you do? Played guitar. What did you eat? Fish and chips. Stories should be very short but very memorable.

Important Rule: You cannot repeat any detail of any story. So, each person must be different, as well as each meeting location, activity, and food. There can be no duplicates among your ten people. You also can't have any common words for the same person. For example, you cannot say you met John Lennon at Lennon University and you played with the little Lennons and ate John Lennon pie. No word in the details of one story can be the same!

Players write the name of their "Who?" in the first column. It doesn't have to be someone famous, but it must be a real name (the name can't be the letter "X," for example). The second column is for the "Where?" This could be a concert, a city, a restaurant—anything goes, but it must be a real place. The third column is for the activity done with each person. Again, must be a real activity. Finally, the fourth column is for the specific food you ate with each person.

Note: By "real," we mean that it can't be gibberish that you've made up! You want other players to remember your stories, and that will be hard to do if they've never heard the words before. But fictional people, places, and activities are fair game, so if you want to ride dinosaurs with Harry Potter, go right ahead!

Players do this ten times and should now have ten rows completed, with a total of forty details that people must try to remember (four details per row).

One player is responsible for writing down the names of each player in the game on an individual piece of paper or index card, mixing them up, and placing them face-down on the table. Before he places it on the table, however, he must remove the name of the player who is going first (Player 1). Next, the player must also write the numbers one to ten on ten separate pieces of paper, mix those up, and place them face-down in a pile next to the pile of names.

OBJECTIVE:

To write ten memorable stories and to remember the details of everyone else's stories when put on the spot.

GAME TIME:

Player 1 plays his card first. All other players' cards are turned over. No pens are allowed for Player 1's entire turn. Player 1 has only five minutes to share the details of each of his ten encounters with the group, without showing his card to anyone! He can tell each of his stories two or three times if he can get them in. However, Player 1 must consider that he scores based on the memory of all the players, and everyone else scores based on how well they remember his stories. Therefore, he must make sure that *everyone* is getting all the details. Again, he cannot show his card to anyone; he simply reads the number and then which story belongs to the number. For example, he will start by saying, "Number 1. John Lennon. Met him at a Beatles concert. We played guitar. We ate fish and chips. Number 2. Elvis Presley. Met him in Nashville. We sang karaoke and ate squid," and so on. Once Player 1 finishes going over all the details of all ten people on his list, he can repeat it and answer questions for people who are trying to remember each one until five minutes are up. When the timer goes off, everything must stop!

Now there are two mixed-up piles face-down in front of him. One pile includes the names of everyone in the game except for his own. The other includes cards with the numbers one to ten.

Player 1 draws a card from the top of the pile of names and then draws a number. Let's say he draws Jack and the number four. Thirty seconds are now put on the clock and Jack must give all the details of the number four person on Player 1's card. Nobody can help him, *especially* not Player 1. Everyone remains silent as Jack tries to answer the name, place, activity, and food on row four of Player 1's card. If he gets it right within the thirty seconds, both Jack and Player 1 get 10 points! Jack must get *all* of the details right! There is no partial credit in this game if players only remember some of the details. If Jack gets it wrong, both Jack and Player 1 lose 10 points! Whether right or wrong, Jack is done playing for now and his name is placed in a new "Bonus Points" pile.

Now, if Jack got it wrong, Player 1 can now recuperate some points for row four by pulling another random name from the hat. The person he picks has a choice. He can go for 5 points if he knows the details of row four, or he can pass. If he goes for it and answers correctly, he and Player 1 get 5 points. If he goes for it and answers incorrectly, he and Player 1 lose 5 points. Either way, his name is placed back in the main pile and row four is now done. Player 1 circles row four and places that number on the side.

Player 1 then picks another name out of the main pile, and another number, and repeats this process. Let's say he picks Laura and row seven. If Laura gets the details of row seven right, she and Player 1 get 10 points. If she gets the details wrong, she and Player 1 lose 10 points. Either way, Laura's name is now placed in the "Bonus Points" pile with Jack.

If she got it wrong, her name and Jack's name are now mixed up in the "Bonus Points" pile and Player 1 randomly picks one of the two. That person gets to decide whether to go for the 5 points or not. If Player 1 picks Laura, most likely she will decline since she just got it wrong. However, Jack now has another chance to get back some points if he was wrong on his first turn.

Note: Jack was the first to go, so Player 1 had to pick from the main pile the first time to determine who would have the choice of going for the 5 points. After the first turn, Player 1 simply picks from the "Bonus Points" pile when that opportunity comes up.

This process keeps repeating, with everyone getting one turn for 10 points and moving from the main pile to the "Bonus Points" pile. Remember, bonus points are only available if the person going for 10 points on his turn gets the details wrong. Then Player 1 makes a random selection from the "Bonus Points" pile. The "Bonus Points" pile keeps growing as the main pile decreases.

Player 1 can gain or lose a lot of points on his turn! It is all a matter of how memorable he made his forty details.

SCORING:

Player 1 keeps track of everyone's scores since nobody else is able to write. He totals everyone's positive and negative points up, and will have a total for the turn.

NEXT:

Player 2 plays her card with her ten stories!

A, B, C, OR D

4+
PLAYERS

//

IT'S ALL IN THE DETAILS!

PREPARATION:

Each player in the game comes up with a fun little story she wants to tell in two minutes or less. The story will be filled with certain details, only one of which will be important. Player 1 will tell her story first. At the end of her story, Player 1 will ask a multiple-choice question and give four possible answers. Everyone else will now have to select the right answer.

> **Note:** In coming up with your story, it is a good idea to think about what your question will be before coming up with the other story details. Write down little notes about your story, your question, and your four answers, and then on your turn to tell your story, you can fill in the rest of the blanks however you like. There's no need to write your whole story down word for word unless you want to. Remember, your story must be a maximum of two minutes long to keep the game moving, and should be at least one minute. Get as creative as you like, but the scoring will dictate your strategy!

OBJECTIVE:

To come up with a story and a question about that story that many people will answer correctly, but not everyone! Also, to answer the other players' questions correctly.

GAME TIME:

Player 1 begins by telling her story. If desired, she can set a timer for two minutes to ensure she doesn't go over. Once she has told her story, she will ask her question and on the count of three, the other players hold up one, two, three, or four fingers to guess the answer. Player 1 reveals the answer, and players note whether they got the answer right. Player 2 then tells his story, and play continues.

SCORING:

The scoring for this game is the key to your storytelling strategy! The guessing players receive 3 points if they answer correctly. If a player answers incorrectly, he receives no points.

Player 1 (the storyteller) receives 2 points for every player who answers her question correctly. However, if *everyone* answers correctly, Player 1 loses points equal to the total number of players in the game. So, with five total players, Player 1 loses 5 points! In addition, if nobody answers correctly, every player guessing receives 3 points and Player 1 still loses 5 points. Therefore, it is important for the storyteller to make her question easy enough for at least one person to get right (preferably many to receive as many points as possible), but not so easy that everyone gets it right.

EXAMPLE:

Player 1 creates a story with a main character named Fred, and there are also several other people in the story. Four of the other people will have a name that also begins with "F."

Her question at the end will be, "How many characters in my story had a name that begins with F? A = 3, B = 4, C= 5, D = 6." The correct answer would be "C." If there are five players guessing and four guess "C," each of those four correct players earns 3 points, and Player 1 earns 8 points (2 points × 4 players).

Player 2 creates a story about all of the places he visited on his trip to Asia and puts in a bunch of details. Then he asks, "Which was the third place I visited? A = Hong Kong, B = Taiwan, C = Malaysia, D = Thailand." Let's say that all players correctly answered "D." All players earn 3 points, but Player 2 loses 5 points for having too easy of a question. Player 2 would also lose 5 points if nobody had answered correctly.

COUPLES CONCENTRATION

A FUN GROUP TWIST ON THIS CLASSIC MEMORY GAME

PREPARATION:

All players create two grids of eight columns and five rows, resulting in forty boxes each, on two separate sheets of paper. Write numbers one through eight along the top from left to right, and letters A through E down the left side for the rows. In the first grid, each player places twenty "couples" somewhere in the grid. (For example, in one box you would put "Romeo," and in another box you would put "Juliet"; in one box you would put "Bonnie," and in another box you would put "Clyde.")

> **Tip:** You can use couples everyone knows in your group, such as friends and family members or famous people, or you can get creative: "Bert and Ernie" could be a couple, or you can even go with "oil and vinegar," "*Star Trek* and *Star Wars*," or "shoes and socks."

The second grid is a scorekeeping grid and remains blank for the time being.

For each grid, players attempt to find more couples than everyone else.

Player 1 starts the game with his grid, and the other players set their grids aside until their round. Like the card game Concentration, every player takes turns asking Player 1 to reveal who is in two specific boxes.

> **Important:** Player 1 should not let any player see his completed game grid at any time during his round. The only grid visible is the scorekeeping grid, which starts out blank until players names are filled in.

Player 2 goes first and asks for two boxes to be revealed by Player 1, one at a time. (For example, Player 2 may first ask for "A4," and Player 1 may reply to the group, "That's 'George Washington,'" and then Player 2 may ask for "C7," and Player 1 may reply to the group, "That's 'Tom Cruise.' No match.") One player at a time asks Player 1 to reveal two boxes. When a player gets a match, he goes again, asking for two more boxes. However, if a player's guess does not turn up a match, play moves on to the next player.

To keep track of the matches and points, Player 1 uses the scorekeeping grid to write the name of the player who got the match in both boxes.

> **Important:** The scorekeeping grid should always be in full view of all the other players. That way, all players know which matches have already been completed and can avoid asking for those specific boxes again.

Once Player 1's grid is completed, round two begins with a new grid from Player 2. Go around the room until all players' grids are guessed, then tally up the points for the final score.

Players earn 1 point for every box they occupy in the scoring grid. Therefore, if a player gets eight matches, he will earn a total of 16 points for that round.

PASS OR NO PASS

4+
PLAYERS

STUMP YOUR FRIENDS IN THIS
TRUE TEST OF MEMORIZATION

PREPARATION:

Every player takes a piece of paper or index card and makes a vertical list of four three-word phrases in large lettering so players across the table can see, numbering them from one to four. Each three-word phrase in this game must include the name of someone in the game as the first word and follow the same "Person's Adjective Noun" pattern.

Example:

1. Brian's Large Mustache
2. Kelly's Crazy Uncle
3. Lindsay's Beautiful Armpit
4. Anthony's Amazing Anteater

Be creative and write legibly! Players can use the same person for more than one phrase or even all four, but at least one word in each phrase must be different.

On the back of the card, players must write their name in large lettering, so all players can see it. Each player then holds her card up with her name facing outward.

One at a time, beginning with Player 1, each player takes turns reading a phrase on her card going in order from number one to number four. For example, Player 1 will read her first phrase, then Player 2 will read his first phrase, Player 3 her first phrase, and so on until it gets back to Player 1, who will read her second phrase, and everyone will follow again until every player in the game has read all four of her three-word phrases.

OBJECTIVE:

Players attempt to be the first to go around the room and correctly guess a phrase in the requested position from each player's list.

GAME TIME:

Once all players have read their lists out loud, Player 1 goes first and picks any other player in the game. That player then asks Player 1 to recall one specific phrase from his card. For example, if Player 1 chooses Player 3, then Player 3 might ask, "What is my number four?" Players have only ten seconds to answer the question each time!

If Player 1 correctly recalls the fourth three-word phrase on Player 3's card, Player 3 must say "Pass" and put the card down on the table, name-up so no one can see his list. Player 1 then continues and picks another player, and that player (just like Player 3) asks Player 1 to come up with the three-word phrase in a specific position on her own card. Every time Player 1 guesses correctly, the player whose card it is says "Pass" and puts the card down on the table with the name face-up. Player 1 continues to go around the room until she guesses incorrectly.

When Player 1 fails to guess the correct three-word phrase from a player's card, that player says, "No pass," and the two exchange cards. (For example, let's say Player 4 asked Player 1 to give her the phrase in position two on her card, and Player 1 guessed incorrectly. Player 4 then says, "No pass" and they exchange cards.) Additionally, everyone else who previously said "Pass" to Player 1 gets to pick up their cards again and hold them, name facing out.

Important: When you say "No pass," *do not* shout out the correct answer! The player who got it wrong will see it because you are exchanging cards, and only that player will now know where she was stumped.

The player who said "No pass" then immediately takes Player 1's place, choosing other players and attempting to guess the three-word phrases in the positions requested.

Players keep exchanging cards when a wrong answer is provided. Players must ask about the card they are holding when another player calls on them, even if it isn't their original card. The name on the back will always be in full view, so the guesser knows who originally wrote the list when asked the question.

The first player to successfully go around the room with a "Pass" from every other player wins.

Tip: For an easy pass when you are no longer holding your own original card, you can always pick the person who is holding your original card first on your turn, but the better strategy is to leave your own card for the end. No reason to remind people what any of your phrases are or where they are in your list!

To add a fun twist, incorporate the following "wild card" option:

Every player holds one wild card per game. A wild card allows you to say, "No pass," even if the player gets it right! The wild card is added to this game to give everyone a chance to take at least one turn at guessing, and for players to have the opportunity to prevent someone from winning the game early on when all the phrases and their positions are still fresh in everyone's minds.

For example, let's say Player 1 selects Player 5, and Player 5 asks for the third phrase on his card. Player 1 guesses correctly. Player 5, however, can now use his wild card option and say, "No pass!" Player 5 must now do two things: First, he must announce that he is using his wild card so everyone knows Player 1 got it right and Player 5 has no more wild card option left. Second, Player 5 must now change the phrase in that position and tell everyone what it is!

Let's say the phrase in the number 3 position on the card Player 5 was holding is "Lindsay's beautiful armpit." Player 5 must now cross that out on the card, write the new phrase in its place (the only time pens are allowed once the guessing begins, and only for this purpose), and let everyone know what the replacement phrase is. Player 5 might say something like: "'Lindsay's beautiful armpit' is now 'Kelly's ugly elbow.'" He will then exchange the card with Player 1, and now Player 5 will take his turn to guess.

1) BRIAN'S LARGE MUSTACHE

2) KELLY'S CRAZY UNCLE

3) LINDSAY'S BEAUTIFUL ARMPIT

4) ANTHONY'S AMAZING ANTEATER

KELLY

TRY TO REMEMBER

PHOTOGRAPHIC MEMORY

3+
PLAYERS

//

WHICH PICTURES WEREN'T IN THE ORIGINAL DRAWING?

PREPARATION:

Each player draws a picture containing ten different objects and nothing else. The objects can be anything: an apple, a man, the sun, the moon, a nose, a candle, a box, a cat, a wizard, and so on. Each object must be different, and no two objects should look alike. (In other words, each player can draw only one person, one car, one tree, one bush, and one dog. The player's person shouldn't look like their dog, and their tree shouldn't look like their bush, and so on.) Draw each object anywhere on a sheet of paper. Players make the objects as clear as possible (within the scope of their talents), and leave enough room for five other objects of equal size to be added to the picture later on. Players should write their own name clearly at the top of their picture.

Players should also create score cards on a separate sheet of paper. Each player should write the name of every player in the game (including their own) with the numbers one through five below each one, leaving room to create a list of five objects for each player.

TRY TO REMEMBER

Players must find the objects that were added to all of the other pictures and make it difficult for other players to find the new objects in their own pictures.

Players pass their pictures around the table. Give each player sixty seconds to study each picture.

Note: The more players in the game, the more time you can allow for studying the pictures.

Look at all of the objects in the pictures carefully! Continue rotating the drawings until they return to the original artists. Once each paper returns to its owner, players label the ten objects in their pictures. In other words, write "dog" next to the dog, "cat" next to the cat, "apple" next to the apple, and so on. Players can't show anyone their pictures while labeling their objects!

Now, each player adds five new objects to his own picture, without letting anyone see! Remember, players cannot draw an object that looks exactly like another in the picture.

Players must label each new object like the others and write the names of the objects on their score card under their name, in the five spaces provided. This is the answer key for each player's picture. Players should put their picture face-down on the table when they are finished labeling the new objects and adding them to their score card.

Now all the pictures are passed around the table again. While looking at each picture, players should write down the five objects they feel were not in the original picture. Players write those objects under that artist's name on their score card. Once all players are done writing down their guesses for all of the pictures, the score cards should be complete.

TRY TO REMEMBER

Now, one at a time, each original artist places his picture face-up in the center of the table and reveals which five objects were added after the first viewing. Players reveal their guesses and tally points.

SCORING:

For every new object that players guess correctly on someone else's picture, they earn 1 point.

In addition, the original artist receives a point for every object that was missed by another player. (For example, if Player 2 correctly guessed three of Player 1's five added objects, Player 2 earns 3 points and Player 1 earns 2 points for the two objects she missed.)

The player with the most points after one full round wins.

Tip: You can earn a lot of extra points from everyone for your own objects if you disguise them well!

SAMPLE:

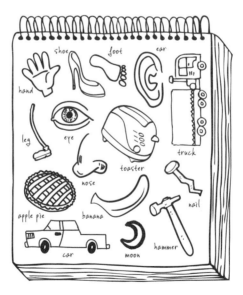

DISTRACTION

3+ PLAYERS

TRY TO FOCUS UNDER IMMENSE PRESSURE

PREPARATION:

Each player in the game writes ten random words on small, separate pieces of paper and mixes them together with everyone else's words, face-down on a table or in a hat where no one can see them. These are the game pieces.

OBJECTIVE:

Under intense pressure, players must remember the words they select each turn.

GAME TIME:

Player 1 goes first and states how many words (anywhere from one to twenty) she wants to remember. Player 2 then draws that many random pieces from the hat. Player 2 must read each word aloud slowly to Player 1. Player 1 *cannot* write the words down!

When Player 2 is done saying the specified number of words, the other players get thirty seconds to distract Player 1 by saying all sorts of other words.

When time is up, Player 2 says, "Silence!" Player 1 must now repeat the words Player 2 said in any order. She has no more than sixty seconds to accomplish this.

If Player 1 remembers all the words, both Player 1 and Player 2 earn points. However, if Player 1 misses any of the words, then Player 1 and Player 2 both lose points. At the end of Player 1's turn, she puts the words back into the hat and mixes them up. Player 2 now gets to choose how many words he wants to remember, and Player 3 will draw exactly that many words from the hat and read them aloud. Some of the words may be repeats from Player 1's round—that's okay. It's all about Player 2 remembering the words for his turn, and repeat words may even be easier to remember.

Once the last player goes, the round is over, and players begin the next round with a clean slate.

To make it fair, Player 2 tests his memory first in the next round. It is Important to rotate on each round. Player 1 should go last in round two, Player 2 should go last in round three, and so on. In addition, players can change the person who reads the words to a given player on each round by having each person randomly pick a name out of a hat. This way, each player gets to benefit from reading to the players with the best memories in the game and vice versa.

To determine how many points each pair of players will earn or lose, multiply the number of words remembered by itself. (For example, if Player 1 attempted and remembered five words, both she and Player 2, the player who read the list to Player 1, would earn 25 points: 5 × 5. On the other hand, if Player 1 messed up and didn't remember all five words, both she and Player 2 would *lose* 25 points!) The player reading the words always receives or loses the same amount of points as the player who succeeds or fails in remembering them.

H ere are four fun puzzles that are fairly easy to make. Each of them will require some thought, but once you get into your groove, you should have no trouble putting them together. Each player in your group can decide which of the four puzzle types he wants to create for everyone else to solve.

Split your group into teams. Begin with the puzzle created by Player 1. First team to solve it wins! Then try the puzzle created by Player 2, and so on.

With a big group, it is a good idea to set a five- to fifteen-minute time limit (depending upon the level of difficulty) for each puzzle. This will typically get everyone motivated and establishes a sense of urgency among the team members. It will also allow for multiple puzzles to be attempted in one group gathering and keeps things fresh if one particular puzzle proves to be too challenging.

MATCH 'EM UP!

3+ PLAYERS

//

PICK A THEME, PICK YOUR TEAMS, AND SEE WHO CAN MAKE ALL THE MATCHES

Tip: A "Match 'Em Up" game board can be created using any of several different themes. The most popular themes are typically movies, TV shows, music, sports, books, or geography, but depending on the interests of the group, there are many more possibilities. This explanation will use movies and actors.

PREPARATION:

The game board consists of two columns. The first column lists twenty movies, and the second lists twenty actors in random order. Each movie must match with one of the actors in the second column.

Tip: There are two ways to make a movie Match 'Em Up puzzle more challenging:

1. Include actors who people may forget were in the movies you have selected.
2. Include actors who have been in more than one of your selected movies.

Similarly, for sports, you might list athletes in one column and their matching teams in the other, but to

I'M PUZZLED

make it more challenging, you could include lesser-known players of a sport and/or players who have played on more than one of the teams in the other column.

GAME TIME:

Show the game board to the teams in your group at the same time. The first team to figure out all twenty matches wins.

SAMPLE PUZZLE

Movies:

1. *A Few Good Men*
2. *Bruce Almighty*
3. *Horrible Bosses*
4. *The Dark Knight Rises*
5. *Pulp Fiction*
6. *Unforgiven*
7. *Cocktail*
8. *Shrek*
9. *The Mask*
10. *Beverly Hills Cop*
11. *Driving Miss Daisy*
12. *Get Shorty*
13. *Top Gun*
14. *Trading Places*
15. *The Cider House Rules*
16. *There's Something about Mary*
17. *Pretty Woman*
18. *Steel Magnolias*
19. *The Color of Money*
20. *Saving Private Ryan*

Actors:

A. Paul Giamatti
B. Matt Dillon
C. Meg Ryan
D. Gene Hackman
E. Kelly Lynch
F. Kevin Bacon
G. Eddie Murphy
H. Charlize Theron
I. Jennifer Aniston
J. Tom Cruise
K. Steve Carell
L. Jason Alexander
M. Anne Hathaway
N. Julia Roberts
O. Morgan Freeman
P. Cameron Diaz
Q. Judge Reinhold
R. Jim Carrey
S. Bruce Willis
T. Dan Aykroyd

I'M PUZZLED

1-F

2-K

3-I

4-M

5-S

6-O

7-E

8-P

9-R

10-Q

11-T

12-D

13-C

14-G

15-H

16-B

17-L

18-N

19-J

20-A

I'M PUZZLED

TRIPLETS

3+ PLAYERS

//

FIND ALL THE GROUPS OF THREE IN A CROWDED LIST!

PREPARATION:

Make a "Triplets" puzzle by creating fifteen groups of three related words. For example, one group of related words might be "bat," "diamond," and "glove" (things related to baseball). Another group might be "basketball," "football," and "rainfall" (words that end with "all"). Another group might be "mitten," "hat," and "sneaker" (things you wear). Yet another group might be "cat," "rat," and "fat" (words that rhyme).

These examples might seem easy to match up. However, when mixed together, the groupings aren't as obvious. (For example, there's a good chance a player may want to put "hat" with "cat" and "rat," or "glove" with "mitten" and "hat.")

This puzzle should be hard enough that players have to think about the different combinations and why certain words may go together. Players may create combinations that simply require some thought, but they might also include words in each three-word group that could fit into several combinations.

I'M PUZZLED

Once the player creating the game board has all fifteen groups, he mixes all of the words into a master list of forty-five words.

Players must find the fifteen triplet groups within the master list.

SAMPLE PUZZLE

Lived	Battleship	Adagio	Rye
Jackson	Splash	Salinger	Superdome
Cranium	Scruples	Skateboard	Viper
Chalet	Decal	Jazz	Rattlesnake
Racket	Boa	Rice	Fitzgerald
Kayak	Wow	Ranch	Wilson
Yale	Skinny	Skyscraper	Crescendo
Row	Garter	Columbia	Taboo
Cleats	Helmet	Flow	Stats
Soprano	Tudor	Creole	
Wheat	Sail	Steinbeck	
French	Madison	Butter	

A. Lived B. Decal C. Flow (Words backward and forward)

A. Skyscraper B. Skateboard C. Skinny (Sk- words)

A. Kayak B. Wow C. Stats (Palindromes)

A. Boa B. Garter C. Viper (Snakes)

A. Creole B. Jazz C. Superdome (New Orleans)

A. Rice B. Columbia C. Yale (Universities)

A. Wheat B. Rye C. French (Bread)

A. Fitzgerald B. Steinbeck C. Salinger (Authors)

A. Taboo B. Scruples C. Cranium (Board games)

A. Tudor B. Ranch C. Chalet (Houses)

A. Jackson B. Wilson C. Madison (Presidents)

A. Helmet B. Racket C. Cleats (Sports equipment)

A. Battleship B. Butter C. Rattlesnake (Words with a double-T)

A. Row B. Splash C. Sail (Things done in water)

A. Soprano B. Adagio C. Crescendo (Music terms)

I'M PUZZLED

PREPARATION:

Draw a grid with six rows and six columns for a total of thirty-six boxes. Think of nine names (first and last) of well-known people, and make sure the first and last names are a combined eight letters or more. Write the names on slips of paper, then chop up each name into four pieces of at least two letters each.

For example, the name "Oprah Winfrey" "chopped up" could have the following pieces:

1. OP
2. RAH
3. WIN
4. FREY

The name "Quentin Tarantino" chopped up could be:

1. QU
2. ENTI

3. NTARA

4. NTINO

Now take all of the thirty-six chopped-up pieces of all nine names and place them randomly in the thirty-six different squares in the grid.

Players from each team must match up the pieces and figure out the nine famous people. The first team to put all the pieces back together, figuratively speaking, wins!

> **Tip:** Nine names can be difficult, so you may want to start with four names using a grid of four rows and four columns with a total of sixteen boxes. Then graduate to the bigger grid!

SAMPLE PUZZLE:

ARLI	AGG	BRO	STRO	INST	TON
OMI	EIN	ZETHE	PLA	ER	NAJO
NJA	AN	ERTE	NG	RON	LLC
JO	BI	CIDOD	YDE	LARM	MES
ALB	HNN	LE	MI	PP	NGO
CH	NEI	GELI	LIN	CKJ	LIE

I'M PUZZLED

1. Johnny Depp
2. Angelina Jolie
3. Charlize Theron
4. Neil Armstrong
5. Bill Clinton
6. Placido Domingo
7. Mick Jagger
8. Lebron James
9. Albert Einstein

I'M PUZZLED

WHAT'S MISSING?

FILL IN THE BLANKS WITH THE RIGHT GROUP OF LETTERS

PREPARATION:

Separate a sheet of paper into two columns with a line or fold. Make a numbered list from one to ten on the left side of the paper, leaving plenty of room to the right of each number. In the column on the right, make a lettered list from A to J.

Next, come up with ten random words. Each word should be at least six letters long. In the list on the left, draw blanks next to each number representing the letters in each word. Write in the letters over the blanks, but leave out *four letters* of each word. Keep each set of four letters together (in any order) and place them in the lettered list in the right-hand column.

> **Tip:** Don't necessarily write the four missing letters directly across from their matching words. Mix them up by placing each group in a different row.

GAME TIME:

The first team to figure out all the words in the left column wins!

1.	B_T_E_F_Y	**A.**	PLEO
2.	_H_W_ _	**B.**	REOF
3.	_ _A_PO_	**C.**	URLT
4.	FO_ _ _ A_L	**D.**	YAER
5.	_O_D_ _	**E.**	ATHC
6.	_L_IM_ _ E	**F.**	HOSM
7.	_RC_I_E_T	**G.**	LIYH
8.	G_ _M_N_	**H.**	ERSO
9.	P_ O _ _SS_R	**I.**	OTLB
10.	_O_ _ DA_	**J.**	UATT

SAMPLE PUZZLE ANSWERS:

1. 1C: Butterfly

2. 2H: Shower

3. 3F: Shampoo

4. 4I: Football

5. 5A: Poodle

6. 6J: Ultimate

7. 7E: Architect

8. 8D: Germany

9. 9B: Professor

10. 10G: Holiday

I'M PUZZLED

None of the first 100 games in this book require any props or materials other than paper and writing instruments and, until now, none of the games have required any real physical activity. So, how do you create a game that will allow the athletes in your group to thrive, but will also allow people of all ages and physical abilities to participate and have fun? I call it Socialympics!

///

CONCENTRATION, COORDINATION, AND SPEED

PREPARATION:

Break up your group into two teams and select ten activities from the list below, or invent your own. These activities will all involve some kind of ball. We find a tennis ball works really well, but you can try many others. The time limit for each of these activities is one minute! Each team takes a turn competing to achieve the maximum amount of exchanges possible within the minute. Be sure to switch off which team goes first in each round to keep things fair.

Activities List

1. **30-Foot Two-Hand Ball Toss:** Two players are 30 feet apart, tossing a ball to each other as many times as possible. Players may use one or two hands to catch the ball. Only completed catches count.

2. **30-Foot One-Hand Ball Toss:** Two players are 30 feet apart, tossing a ball to each other as many times as possible. Players may *only* use one hand to catch the ball. Only completed catches count.

3. **20-Foot Two-Hand Ball Toss:** Two players are 20 feet apart, tossing a ball to each other as

many times as possible. Players may use one
or two hands to catch the ball. Only completed
catches count.

4. **20-Foot One-Hand Ball Toss:** Two players are
    20 feet apart, tossing a ball to each other as many
    times as possible. Players may *only* use one hand
    to catch the ball. Only completed catches count.

5. **10-Foot Two-Hand Ball Toss:** Two players are
    10 feet apart, tossing a ball to each other as
    many times as possible. Players may use one
    or two hands to catch the ball. Only completed
    catches count.

6. **10-Foot One-Hand Ball Toss:** Two players are
    10 feet apart, tossing a ball to each other as many
    times as possible. Players may *only* use one hand
    to catch the ball. Only completed catches count.

7. **10-Foot One-Hand Ball Toss Switch:** Two players
    are 10 feet apart, tossing a ball to each other as
    many times as possible. Players catch the ball
    with one hand, pass or hand the ball to their other
    hand, and throw with that hand. It doesn't matter
    which hand catches the ball each time as long as
    players throw with the hand that didn't catch the
    ball. If the player throws with the same hand, the
    other player's catch doesn't count. Only completed
    catches count.

8. **10-Foot Behind-the-Back Toss:** Two players are
    10 feet apart, tossing a ball to each other as many
    times as possible. Players catch the ball with one
    hand, then put it behind their back and transfer
    to the other hand, and then toss it back to their
    partner. It doesn't matter which hand catches the
    ball each time as long as they put it behind their
    back and transfer it to their other hand. Players
    must throw the ball with the hand to which it was

transferred. If players transfer in front or throw with the hand that just caught the ball, the other player's catch doesn't count. Only completed catches count.

9. **20-Foot Knee Toss (Soft Surface):** Two players are 20 feet apart, tossing a ball to each other as many times as possible while on their knees. Players may use one or two hands to catch the ball. Players must have both knees on the ground when they throw and catch the ball. Only completed catches count. Players can stand up and retrieve any ball missed, but then must get back on their knees before throwing again.

10. **20-Foot Cross-Legged Toss:** Two players are 20 feet apart, tossing a ball to each other as many times as possible while sitting cross-legged. Players may use one or two hands to catch the ball. Players must be sitting cross-legged when they throw and catch the ball. Only completed catches count. They can stand up and get any ball missed, but then must sit back down before throwing again.

11. **Back-to-Back Handoff:** Two players stand back-to-back, transferring the ball to each other as many times as possible. Player 1 sticks out his right hand to take the ball from Player 2, who gives it with her left hand. Player 1 transfers the ball from his right to his left hand, then passes it to Player 2's right hand. Player 2 passes the ball from her right to her left hand, then passes it back to Player 1's right hand. Each time someone receives the ball counts as one catch. (Right and left can be switched around according to players' preference—the important part is that players remain back-to-back the entire time!)

12. **30-Foot Two-Hand Bounce:** Two players are 30 feet apart, bouncing a ball to each other as many times as possible. Players may use one or two hands to catch the ball. Only completed catches count, and only one bounce! More than one bounce doesn't count.

13. **10-Foot, Facing Away, Under-the-Leg Roll:** Two players are 10 feet apart, bent over, facing away from each other, tossing a ball under their legs back and forth as many times as possible. Players can roll or bounce the ball, and there is no limit to how many bounces. Each player must catch it and then toss it back. Players can use one or two hands to catch the ball. Only completed catches count. If the ball is dropped or even rolls away from the player's hands after they touch it, it doesn't count.

14. **20-Foot Facing Away, Under-the-Leg Roll:** Two players are 20 feet apart, bent over, facing away from each other, tossing a ball under their legs back and forth as many times as possible. Players can roll or bounce the ball, and there is no limit to how many bounces. Each player must catch it and then toss it back. Players can use one or two hands to catch the ball. Only completed catches count. If the ball is dropped or even rolls away from the player's hands after they touch it, it doesn't count.

15. **10-Foot Kick (Hard Surface):** Two players are 10 feet apart, kicking a ball back and forth to each other as many times as possible. Players don't have to stop the ball before kicking again. However, if the ball doesn't make it to the other person because of a weak kick, it doesn't count. Players must kick from at least 10 feet away. If the kick doesn't make it to the other person, the kicker

must retrieve the ball, return to 10 feet away, and re-kick it for the kick to count.

16. **Back-to-Back Over-the-Head Toss (Not advisable indoors with a low ceiling):** Two players are standing back-to-back, tossing the ball over their heads as many times as possible. Players must throw the ball over their heads while standing back-to-back. As long as a player starts back-to-back on the throw and the throw is directly over her head, her partner can separate herself to make the catch. So, if players need to move forward to make the catch, it is fine. They must then get back to the starting position to make another throw. Only completed catches count.

17. **5-Foot Under-the-Leg, One-Hand Toss and Catch:** Two players are standing 5 feet apart, tossing the ball underneath each other's legs back and forth as many times as possible. Players must stand with their feet apart, facing their partner, and toss and catch the ball with one hand by reaching in between both legs from behind. Players must toss and catch the ball from this position. Only completed catches count. Players must always be at least 5 feet apart on both the toss and catch.

18. **Lying-Down, Feet-Touching Toss:** Two players are lying down on their backs with both of their feet touching and their heads completely on the ground, tossing the ball back and forth as many times as possible. Players' heads must be on the ground when they toss and catch to their partner. A catch does not count if their head comes off the ground. Players may stand up to get a ball which was missed or dropped, but cannot throw

it until they are back in position. Only completed catches count.

19. **Lying-Down, Elbows-on-Ground 10-Foot Toss (Soft Surface):** Two players are lying down on their stomachs with elbows touching the ground, 10 feet apart, and tossing the ball back and forth as many times as possible. Players must be in this position with their elbows touching the ground when they throw and catch. A catch does not count if even one elbow comes off the ground. Players may stand up to get a ball that was missed or dropped, but they cannot throw it until they are back in position with both elbows on the ground. Only completed catches count.

20. **30-Foot Handoff Relay Race:** Set up an object 30 feet from the starting line. One of the two players starts with the ball, runs to that object and touches it, then runs back to the starting line. He hands the ball off to his partner, who then runs to the object and back handing the ball back to her partner, who repeats the process. The goal is for the two players to complete as many handoffs as possible within the sixty seconds. Players must always hand the ball off to their partner behind the starting line before their partner can run again. Each handoff counts. If players drop the ball on the handoff, that exchange doesn't count!

Note: For all of these events, the one-minute timer never stops. If a ball skips far away, you simply need to go retrieve it as quickly as possible and get back into position before you can continue. Nobody can help you get the ball. You must do this yourself!

Once players decide on the ten events that will be included in the competition, it is now important to organize who will compete in each event. With four total players (two per team), everyone will compete in all ten events. However, with more than two players on a team, each player on the team must compete in at least two events, but no more than eight. This rule could significantly affect which events players decide to include in the competition. It will also affect the decision as to who should be partners in each event, and which combinations of players overall will be the most competitive.

> **Note:** Once you determine who will compete in all ten events, your team lineup of partners for each event should be exchanged with the other team. No substitutions are allowed once the lineups have been exchanged, with the exception of injury.

The scoring for this competition is also going to significantly play into your strategy. In every one of the ten events, your team is looking to achieve the maximum ten points by recording more catches in one minute than your opponent. If your team records more catches, your team gets 10 points. The other team gets 10 minus the score differential. For example, for the "30-Foot Two-Hand Ball Toss," let's say Team A recorded forty catches and team B recorded thirty-six catches. Team A would get 10 points and Team B would get 6 points. (10 minus 4 for Team B). Let's then say that for the "10-Foot Under-the-Leg Roll," Team B recorded twenty-six catches and Team A recorded eighteen catches. Team B would get 10 points and Team A would get 2 points. (10 minus 8 for Team A.) The ultimate goal with each event is to obtain a shutout! That would mean you caught at least ten more balls than the other team. Ten to zero is the best you can do. There are no negative points for the other team if you win by more than 10 points. This keeps the competition fair and allows the other team to be able to catch up if they were particularly weak in an event, or if the other team was just that much stronger—or perhaps something went terribly wrong! Many circumstances could factor into a major win or loss in an event. Knowing that you can only lose by a maximum of 10 points could play into how you match up your teammates.

In conclusion, your best score is 100 if you win all ten events. If there is a tie in an event, both teams get 10 points. If there is an overall tie at the end of all ten events, a "30-Foot Handoff Relay" is organized. You may select any two players on your team to run the relay as described in event twenty above. However, for this relay, there is no one-minute timer. The stopwatch is set to record how fast each team can complete twenty-five handoffs. The clock is stopped once the twenty-fifth handoff is completed.

THANK YOU! THANK YOU! THANK YOU!

A special thanks to all of the social gamers in my never-ending focus group who have volunteered through the years to have a ton of fun and make this book possible!

Taylor, Rebekah, Barbara, Jerry, Michael, Meri, Lesly, Graham, Ridley, Lindsay, Brian, Greta, Eva, Rocky, Lisa, Levon, Kelly, Anthony C., Georgia, Kevin, Jill, Abe, Richie, David, Osie, Marvin, Rose, Jim, Jud, Janine, Jess W., Marc I., Anthony P., Neil, Debbie, Louis, Danny, Cynthia, Billy, Rich R., Brandt, Amy, Diana, Jennifer K., Jennifer P., Mike S., Ray V., Devin, Phil, Megan, Matt, Danielle, Nadia, Nicole, Jim L., Kirsten, Wendy, Thomas, Russell, Bob, Emily, Chip, Shane . . . and many more.

BRAD BERGER grew up in Great Neck, New York. He attended the University of Colorado, where he earned a degree in French, Italian, and German and spent several years living and working in Europe. He currently resides on Long Island, where he works as president and publisher of a 130-year-old, family-owned publishing company.

Since his childhood, Brad has enjoyed bringing his friends and family together to play all kinds of games. However, with the invention of so much technology, Brad saw a decline in group-based activities within his own family and circle of friends. Inspired to bring people back together without technological interruption, Brad crafted the ultimate playbook of new games to give people a reason to come together and "unplug" for a while.

Website: www.bradbergergames.com

ABOUT FAMILIUS

Welcome to a place where books—and family—are beautiful. Familius: a book publisher dedicated to helping families be happy. If you feel a few friends and family might benefit from what you've read, let us know and we'll be happy to provide you with quantity discounts. Simply email us at orders@familius.com.

Website: www.familius.com
Facebook: www.facebook.com/paterfamilius
Twitter: @familiustalk, @paterfamilius1
Pinterest: www.pinterest.com/familius